# LISTENING TO GOD

LEARN TO HEAR HIM THROUGH HIS WORD

## CHARLES F. STANLEY

THOMAS NELSON
Since 1798

LISTENING TO GOD
CHARLES F. STANLEY BIBLE STUDY SERIES

Original edition copyright 1996 and 2008 by Charles F. Stanley.
Revised and updated edition copyright 2019 by Charles F. Stanley.

Published in Nashville, Tennessee, by Thomas Nelson. Thomas Nelson is a registered trademark of HarperCollins Christian Publishing, Inc.

All Scripture quotations are taken from the New King James Version.® Copyright © 1982 by Thomas Nelson. Used by permission. All rights reserved worldwide.

Thomas Nelson titles may be purchased in bulk for educational, business, fundraising, or sales promotional use. For information, e-mail SpecialMarkets@ThomasNelson.com.

ISBN 978-0-310-10659-3

First Printing August 2019 / Printed in the United States of America
23 24 25 26 27  LBC  17 16 15 14 13

# CONTENTS

# PREPARING TO HEAR FROM GOD

God spoke to His prophets in Old Testament times, giving them specific messages for themselves and for His people as a whole. Many Christians in modern times, however, believe that God no longer speaks to His people as He once did. But this is not the case! God is still speaking to His people—to all His people, not just those who are specially selected as His spokespersons. He speaks through our times of prayer, through counsel from wise Christians, and most importantly, through His Word, the Bible.

The Bible is God's foremost method of communication with us today. It is the wellspring from which new insights and eternal wisdom come to us. It is the reference to which we must return continually to check out messages that we believe are from God.

This book can be used by you alone or by several people in a small-group study. At various times, you will be asked to relate to the material in one of the following four ways.

*First, what new insights have you gained?* Make notes about the insights you have. You may want to record them in your Bible or in a separate journal. As you reflect on your insights, you are likely to see how God has moved in your life.

*Second, have you ever had a similar experience?* You approach the Bible from your own unique background . . . your own particular set of understandings about the world that you bring with you when you open God's Word. For this reason, it is important to consider how your experiences are shaping your understanding and allow yourself to be open to the truth that God reveals.

*Third, how do you feel about the material?* While you should not depend solely on your emotions as a gauge for your faith, it is important for you to be aware of your feelings as you study a passage of Scripture and have the freedom to express your emotions to God. Sometimes, the Holy Spirit will use your emotions to compel you to look at your life in a different or challenging way.

*Fourth, in what way do you feel challenged to respond or to act?* God's Word may inspire you or challenge you to take a particular action. Take this challenge seriously and find ways to move into it. If God reveals a particular need that He wants you to address, take that as His "marching orders." God will empower you to do something with the challenge that He has just given you.

Start your Bible study sessions in prayer. Ask God to give you spiritual eyes to see and spiritual ears to hear. As you conclude your study, ask the Lord to seal what you have learned so you will not forget it. Ask Him to help you grow into the fullness of the nature and character of Christ Jesus. Again, keep the Bible at the center of your study. A genuine Bible study stays focused on God's Word and promotes a growing faith and a closer walk with the Holy Spirit in each person who participates.

Again, I caution you to keep the Bible at the center of your study. A genuine Bible study stays focused on God's Word and promotes a growing faith and a closer walk with the Holy Spirit in each person who participates.

# GOD HAS SOMETHING TO SAY TO US

## IN THIS LESSON

*Learning:* Does God still speak to people today?

*Growing:* What is the purpose of prayer
and reading the Bible?

One of the most important lessons we can learn is how to listen to God. In this complex, nothing is more urgent, necessary, or more rewarding than hearing what God has to say, both as individuals and as members of the body of Christ. After all, if we want to develop a relationship with another person, we have to converse with that person in some manner. This means both talking *and* listening.

Most of us do better with the talking part. In my own life, I remember a time when I was too occupied doing the Lord's work to pay close attention to God's voice. I was preaching six times a week, taping two television programs, traveling across the nation, writing a book, pastoring the church, and administrating a large church staff and broadcast ministry, among other daily duties. In the midst of it all, I spent time *talking* to God—often about the needs I was facing in my personal life and ministry—but not much time *listening* to God. I ended up in the hospital for a week and out of circulation for three months. The net result for each of us, if we don't learn how to listen to God, is that we will make unwise and costly mistakes.

You may ask, "Does God really speak to us today?" The Bible assures us that He does. The book of Hebrews opens this way "God, who at various times and in various ways spoke in time past to the fathers by the prophets, has in these last days spoken to us by His Son, whom He has appointed heir of all things, through whom also He made the worlds" (Hebrews 1:1-2).

Our God is not a speechless God. He is alive and active in our world today. He speaks! The primary goal of any communicator is not to speak well but to be heard. God speaks in a way we can hear Him, receive His message, and understand what He wants us to do.

**1.** The author of Hebrews states that "in these last days," God has "spoken to us by His Son" (Hebrews 1:2). What does the author mean by these statements?

**2.** How does God speak to people today? How has He spoken to you in the past?

..................................................................................................

..................................................................................................

..................................................................................................

..................................................................................................

..................................................................................................

# GOD'S PERSONAL WORD

God speaks in both general and absolute terms to all people, and He speaks to each one of us personally. We can hardly comprehend that possibility with our finite minds. God is an infinite God, and He is capable of communicating with each one of us, right where we are. He can speak to us in the midst of our circumstances or crises—in personal, direct, and explicit terms.

This may be the most important concept that we can ever grasp when it comes to learning how to listen to God. When God speaks, He is speaking directly to us. Everything in the Bible applies to our lives in some way. Every message based on the Word of God has truth embedded within it that is for our lives. There is no such thing as a chapter in the Bible, a sermon based on God's Word, or a book that expounds and explains God's Word that is not for us.

Now, the question is whether we truly consider the Bible this way—as God's communication with us—and value it in this manner. I always laugh when I hear people say their Bible is still like new, because what they just did is confess they are not reading it and applying it to their situation. If we don't ever open up the Bible and read it—get it all broken in and marked up—it's going to be difficult to lead a godly life. When we truly begin to understand the benefits and the value of the Bible, it doesn't stay looking like new for very long.

How you and I handle something depends on the value we place on it. For example, no one who likes to go fishing would ever purchase a high-end rod and just hang it up as a decoration on their wall. No, they would take it out, learn all they could about how it works, and take it with them on their next trip out to catch fish. When they returned home, they wouldn't take the rod and just toss it over into the corner somewhere. Rather, they would clean it, wipe it down, polish it, and oil it up a bit to make sure it's ready for the next trip.

The same is true of God's Word. If we don't consider it as being valuable to us, we will lay it up on a shelf somewhere, or maybe bring it to church, or just ignore it until it's covered with dust. But if we view God's Word as "living and powerful, and sharper than any two-edged sword, piercing even to the division of soul and spirit" (Hebrews 4:12), we will understand it is not like any other book. There is no book to match the Bible because it represents the very mind of God put into print. As we open its pages, we learn to know the ways of God, comprehend His character, and hear His voice speaking into our lives.

**3.** "He who is of God hears God's words; therefore you do not hear, because you are not of God" (John 8:47). Why is it important to open up God's Word to have a vibrant relationship with Him?

................................................................................

................................................................................

................................................................................

................................................................................

................................................................................

**4.** What value would you say you place on God's Word? Is reading the Bible a part of your everyday life? Or is it just something you bring to church on Sunday? Explain.

................................................................................

................................................................................

................................................................................

................................................................................

................................................................................

# GOD'S GUIDING VOICE

In Psalm 119:105, we read, "Your word is a lamp to my feet and a light to my path." When we want to discover God's direction for our lives, one of the simplest things we can do is get into the Word of God. Whenever we are struggling to make a decision, one of the first things we do is call our friends. We share our situation and our problems with them, and we ask for them to give us advice. However, when we are looking for direction, the best place to go first is to the Word of God. Our friends may be able to give us good advice, but the Word of God will always give us the *correct* advice—and it is absolutely complete.

God is so willing to communicate His will to us today. He has provided His Word, the Bible, as a lamp to light our way in this life. People often say the Bible is a "mystery book." They complain it's filled with stories from a long time ago that are so unfamiliar to them. They have trouble comprehending how it can guide their lives. But the truth is that when we go to God and ask Him for clarity, He will reveal some verses that communicate His will to us.

As the psalmist notes, "Through Your precepts I get understanding; therefore I hate every false way" (Psalm 119:104). We become wise by getting into the Scripture, asking God to guide us as we read, listening for His direction, and then acting on that instruction. As we read the Bible and allow it to transform our minds, we begin to think the way God thinks. The Bible is a highly personal book, and each of us must take God's Word personally!

Of course, this is not to say that God has an *exclusive* word for a person. God doesn't deal in secrets. He won't reveal truth to one person and deny it to another. Be on guard if you hear somebody say, "God told me something, but He told me that I can't tell anybody else," or, "God had a word that's just for me and not for you." God doesn't play favorites. He doesn't speak to one child and totally ignore His other children. His word of correction to you may be so personal that you don't want to share it with others, but God's word of correction is an absolute that applies to all people. The same goes for God's promises, provisions, and insights.

**5.** "If any of you lacks wisdom, let him ask of God, who gives to all liberally and without reproach, and it will be given to him" (James 1:5). When are some times that you sought God's wisdom by engaging in His Word? What happened as a result?

.................................................................................................

.................................................................................................

.................................................................................................

.................................................................................................

**6.** How has God has personally guided you through His Word?

.................................................................................................

.................................................................................................

.................................................................................................

.................................................................................................

## GOD'S COMFORTING VOICE

In Psalm 119:28, the psalmist writes, "My soul melts from heaviness; strengthen me according to Your word." When we are grieved in our spirit and are hurting, we are reminded in the Bible that God loves us, cares for us, and is personally interested in us. As God communicates this truth to us through the pages of Scripture, our grief turns to a sense of peace and joy, and we find the strength to persevere. Such is the power of the Word of God.

When we read of God's love for us, and understand His power, and comprehend the way He works in our lives, our sadness turns to joy because we realize God is living inside of us. It is for this very reason that Paul could write, "Rejoice in the Lord always. Again I will say, rejoice!" (Philippians 4:4). No matter what we are facing, when we have a relationship with Christ we find that somehow we have a deep sense of abiding joy. It is a joy that is unspeakable and indescribable . . . a joy that is beyond anything we can muster within ourselves or manufacture by anything we can do. It is not "mind over matter." It is the gift of God.

Jesus said, "Peace I leave with you, My peace I give to you; not as the world gives do I give to you. Let not your heart be troubled, neither let it be afraid" (John 14:27). God's voice comforts us in even the stormiest times of life—moments when the bottom drops out, the sides cave in, the top falls in, and we wonder where our friends have gone. It's like a stream of peace that runs at a deeper level than our lives. We can't put our finger on it—but we can sense it is there. It is a peace that surpasses all human understanding and guards our hearts and our minds (see Philippians 4:7).

7. "You will keep him in perfect peace, whose mind is stayed on You, because he trusts in You" (Isaiah 26:3). How does reading God's Word keep your mind "stayed" on God? How does this result in trusting God . . . and greater peace in your life?

8. How has God comforted you through His Word and brought you greater peace?

13

# GOD'S PURPOSEFUL VOICE

God doesn't speak frivolously. He doesn't joke around. God means what He says and will do what He says. As we read in Numbers 23:19:

> God is not a man, that He should lie, nor a son of man, that He should repent. Has He said, and will He not do? Or has He spoken, and will He not make it good?

God is serious about His relationship with you. He doesn't speak to you in idle terms. He expects you to respond to His voice, heed His Word, and act on it.

Can you remember last Sunday's sermon? Can you recall what you read in God's Word yesterday? You will be able to remember if you are listening for what God has to say to you and if you take seriously the idea that God wants you to do something in response to His Word. As James writes, "Be doers of the word, and not hearers only, deceiving yourselves" (1:22).

God speaks for your benefit. He wants you to listen to Him and respond to His words. Sometimes He will challenge you to change your thinking or to release certain feelings and opinions that you have been harboring. Sometimes He will command you to change certain aspects of your behavior. Sometimes He will just want to encourage you so that you might live your life with greater joy and strength—and greater peace. Always, however, God's Word is for your transformation. It is intended to change you in some way.

As you go through this study, approach God's Word seriously and listen for what He is saying to you. Listening to God is not a casual pastime or a "let's try it and see if you like it" activity. Listening to God is the most important thing you can do for your eternal future.

**9.** "There are many plans in a man's heart, nevertheless the LORD's counsel—that will stand" (Proverbs 19:21). When are some times

that God has changed your plans? How did He make you aware
that He was guiding you in a different direction?

..........................................................................................................

..........................................................................................................

..........................................................................................................

..........................................................................................................

**10.** How could you strengthen your relationship with God today to
improve your communication?

..........................................................................................................

..........................................................................................................

..........................................................................................................

..........................................................................................................

## TODAY AND TOMORROW

*Today:* God speaks today—and He wants to speak to me.

*Tomorrow:* I will spend time this week listening to God,
reading His Word, and speaking to Him.

# CLOSING PRAYER

*God, thank You that You speak to us today. We praise and bless You for being
so gracious, loving, kind, and willing to hear us. Today, we pray for those who
have never received Christ—and never listened for Your voice. We pray the
Holy Spirit would speak to their hearts the simple truth of the gospel and they
would be aware of Your presence in a real way. In Your name we pray. Amen.*

# NOTES AND PRAYER REQUESTS

· · · · · · · · · · · · · · · · · · · · · · · · · · · · · · · · · · · · · · · · · · ·

Use this space to write any key points, questions, or prayer requests from this week's study.

# WHY GOD SPEAKS TO US

## IN THIS LESSON

*Learning:* Why does God want to communicate
with me personally?

*Growing:* How can I improve that communication?

God speaks to us for reasons that are purely His own: He loves us and desires to have a relationship with us. Asaph, the musician and psalmist, provides this deeply moving plea from God to His people in Psalm 81:8–16:

Hear, O My people, and I will admonish you!
O Israel, if you will listen to Me!
There shall be no foreign god among you;

Nor shall you worship any foreign god.
I am the LORD your God,
Who brought you out of the land of Egypt;
Open your mouth wide, and I will fill it.

But My people would not heed My voice,
And Israel would have none of Me.
So I gave them over to their own stubborn heart,
To walk in their own counsels.

Oh, that My people would listen to Me,
That Israel would walk in My ways!
I would soon subdue their enemies,
And turn My hand against their adversaries.
The haters of the LORD would pretend submission to Him,
But their fate would endure forever.
He would have fed them also with the finest of wheat;
And with honey from the rock I would have satisfied you.

Can you hear the sorrow in God's voice as He pleads with His people to listen to Him? And for what purpose? So He might bless them! God wants only good for His people.

God created us for fellowship. He desires to walk and talk with us, just as He did with Adam and Eve. He loves us and wants us to love Him in return. He gives to us and wants us to give back to Him. He shields us from evil and longs for us to trust Him. He provides all that we need and asks that we rely on Him as the source of our total supply. He is our Father, and we are His children. He desires that our relationship be healthy, joyful, loving, and fulfilling.

Specifically, God desires that we *comprehend* His truth. He desires that we *learn* about who He is, who we are, and the relationship He wants to have with us. He desires us to be *conformed* to His truth—to apply His truth to our lives in a way that transforms us more closely into the image of Christ Jesus. And God desires us to *communicate* His truth to others.

1. According to Psalm 81:8–16, what must God's people do if they want to hear His voice?

 

 

 

 

2. What does God promise to do for His people if they will obey?

 

 

 

 

## COMPREHENDING GOD'S TRUTH

God has given to all believers a divine person, the Holy Spirit, who lives within us to help us receive and understand the truth. The Holy Spirit knows perfectly the mind of God, and the Holy Spirit communicates to our spirits the truth God wants us to hear. God desires for us to know His mind. Of course, we will never know the mind of God *completely,* because we are finite creatures and He is infinite. But we can grow in our understanding about who God is, how He operates in our world, and why He does the things He does.

For many reasons, we may be limited in our understanding of God's motives and methods. One reason might be because we have never read through the Bible. To understand the true and full context of any passage in God's Word, we need to understand the true and full context of *all* God's Word. Also, we may have cultural differences that keep us from understanding fully what certain things mean in the Bible. We may be trying to understand the Bible solely with our minds, which is always futile. The Bible speaks to our spirit.

None of these reasons, however, are a fixed barrier for us. We can grow in our understanding by reading more of God's Word, studying the cultural background of the Bible, and learning how to read the Bible with spiritual understanding.

**3.** "But the Helper, the Holy Spirit, whom the Father will send in My name, He will teach you all things, and bring to your remembrance all things that I said to you" (John 14:26). What does it mean that the Holy Spirit will "bring to your remembrance" the words of Jesus? What is required of you for Jesus' words to be brought back to your memory?

**4.** What are some barriers you have encountered when it comes to comprehending the truth of God's Word? What have you done to address those issues?

# LEARNING THE TRUTH
# ABOUT GOD AND OURSELVES

The Lord desires for us to learn three major truths about Himself. *The first is that He is our Creator.* The opening verse in Scripture proclaims, "In the beginning God created the heavens and the earth" (Genesis 1:1). God fashioned us as unique creatures. He made the natural world for us to rule and enjoy. He has provided all we need.

*The second truth is that God is our life.* The Bible records that God breathed into us His breath: "The Lord God formed man of the dust of the ground, and breathed into his nostrils the breath of life; and man became a living being" (Genesis 2:7). We are spirit because God imparted His Spirit to us. We cannot exist apart from God.

*The third truth is that God loves us.* God is continually reaching out to us with affection. "For God so loved the world that He gave His only begotten Son" (John 3:16). In fact, God's very nature is love, for "God is love" (1 John 4:8). He calls to us individually by name.

Once we come to understand these truths about God, we can then come to learn two important truths about ourselves. *The first truth is that we are all sinners before a holy God and in need of a Savior.* The Scriptures paint a bleak picture of our fallen human state: "For all have sinned and fall short of the glory of God" (Romans 3:23). Jesus even said to a group of Pharisees, who were considered the religious elite of His day, "You are of your father the devil, and the desires of your father you want to do" (John 8:44). The primary message of the Holy Spirit is that we need God.

*The second truth is that God offers us salvation through Christ and the gift of the Holy Spirit, who becomes our Comforter and Counselor.* In 1 Peter 4:18–19, we read, "You were not redeemed with corruptible things . . . from your aimless conduct received by tradition from your fathers, but with the precious blood of Christ, as of a lamb without blemish and without spot." Once we receive the salvation that Jesus offers, we receive the gift of the Holy Spirit, who dwells within us. As Jesus said, "I will pray to the Father, and He will give you another Helper, that He may abide with you forever" (John 14:16).

The Holy Spirit will speak hope to us. He will strengthen our faith and enable us to trust in God. He will give us the assurance of our salvation and God's faithfulness and total provision toward us. He will reveal to us our nature as God's saints on the earth and will challenge us to grow to become more like Jesus. As we discover these truths about ourselves, we will begin to see others in a new light. We will view our fellow believers as those whom God is also fashioning, forming, and transforming. We will see that all people are loved by God, are in need of God, and can have access to God. We become more inclined to love others unconditionally.

5. "Beloved, let us love one another, for love is of God; and everyone who loves is born of God and knows God" (1 John 4:7). God is our creator and our life . . . and He loves us. How does this verse suggest we are to reflect that love to others?

........................................................................................................

........................................................................................................

........................................................................................................

........................................................................................................

........................................................................................................

6. "Therefore, if anyone is in Christ, he is a new creation; old things have passed away; behold, all things have become new" (2 Corinthians 5:17). What does it mean to be a "new creation" in Christ? How does the Holy Spirit help us to be "new creatures"?

........................................................................................................

........................................................................................................

........................................................................................................

........................................................................................................

........................................................................................................

# BEING CONFORMED BY GOD'S TRUTH

It is not enough for us to *comprehend* God's truth—we must also be *conformed* to God's truth. The Lord calls us to present ourselves to Him as if we are a living sacrifice. The apostle Paul writes:

> I beseech you therefore, brethren, by the mercies of God, that you present your bodies a living sacrifice, holy, acceptable to God, which is your reasonable service (Romans 12:1).

In the Old Testament, God consumed sacrifices with His holy fire as a sign of His presence among the people. In our day, God's holy presence burns out everything that is not like Jesus in our lives. God then then causes each of His followers to burn and to shine brightly with a zeal for Him.

As we read and hear God's Word, we come face to face with ourselves, our deficiencies, our errors, and our faults. We say again and again, "I'm not like Jesus . . . but I want to be like Him." At these times, we can know that God is truly speaking to us, because God always calls us to become more and more like Jesus. How do we do this? We simply say to the Father, "Help me to change. Help me to be more like Jesus." God has promised to show us how to be like Jesus and to help us become more like Him.

Each time you realize your life doesn't line up perfectly with the truth of God's Word, you have a choice to make: you can either accept God's way or reject it. When you accept God's way and openly say to the Lord, "I'm not like that, but I want to be like that," He begins to do something inside you. You may find your tastes are changing. You may become uncomfortable in situations in which you used to feel comfortable. You may have new desires for things that are good, healthful, and wholesome. These are signs of the transforming power of God at work!

**7.** "Do not be conformed to this world, but be transformed by the renewing of your mind, that you may prove what is that good and acceptable and perfect will of God" (Romans 12:2). What does it mean to "be conformed to this world"?

..................................................................................................

..................................................................................................

..................................................................................................

..................................................................................................

..................................................................................................

..................................................................................................

..................................................................................................

..................................................................................................

**8.** How does a renewed mind improve a believer's communication with God? How would a Christian's prayers be hindered if he or she is "conformed to this world"?

..................................................................................................

..................................................................................................

..................................................................................................

..................................................................................................

..................................................................................................

..................................................................................................

..................................................................................................

..................................................................................................

# COMMUNICATING GOD'S TRUTH TO OTHERS

God also desires that we communicate His truth to others. He does not give us His truth so we might hoard it but that we might share it. He does not impart blessings so we might store them up but that we might give them away to others and grow in our capacity to receive even more from Him. He does not love us so we might merely bask in His love but that we might extend His love to others. As Jesus commanded, "Go therefore and make disciples" (Matthew 28:19).

You communicate your relationship with God whether you intend to do so or not. Your actions, your demeanor, and your spontaneous words reflect your heart. God wants you to *actively* and *intentionally* share with others what you know about Him. God wants others to come to know Him and for you to continue to grow in Him. He wants you to share so you will have more brothers and sisters in Christ and so your relationship with them will be richer.

God wants you to have a loving relationship with Him as your heavenly Father, and He also desires that you have loving relationships with other people so your life will be more joyful, meaningful, and fulfilling. He doesn't call you to have a relationship with Him in isolation. Rather, He desires for you to become a *family* of God with others on earth.

When you openly and freely share the truth of God with others, you build community. You forge eternal relationships. You connect with people who also are seeking to know God's truth and be conformed to it. In that community, you find strength, comfort, and mutual assistance. You become "fitted together" with others in a bond that collectively brings you toward greater wholeness.

God knows the more you see Him for who He is in His fullness—as your loving Father and Creator who desires only the best for you—the more you are going to want to be with Him. The more you are with Him, the more you are going to want to become like Him. The more you become like Him, the greater your witness will be to others in the world. The greater your witness to others, the more they will begin to hear His voice . . . and the more enriching and loving your relationships will become.

God speaks to you for your benefit—and simply for His own delight in establishing a relationship with you.

**9.** "Therefore comfort each other and edify one another, just as you also are doing" (1 Thessalonians 5:11). The word *edify* in this verse is related to the word *edifice*, which means an impressive building or structure. Given this, what does it mean to *edify* one another? How might you improve another person's communication and relationship with God by edifying him or her?

**10.** "If someone says, 'I love God,' and hates his brother, he is a liar; for he who does not love his brother whom he has seen, how can he love God whom he has not seen?" (1 John 4:20). Why is it important to love other people if you truly want to love God? How might a lack of love for others hinder your individual prayers and communication with God?

## TODAY AND TOMORROW

*Today:* In order to communicate with God, I need to understand the truth about God, myself, and others.

*Tomorrow:* I will spend time this week asking God to reveal the truth to me in greater measure.

# CLOSING PRAYER

*Father, thank You for Your lovingkindness and Your tender mercy toward us. How often we must have had the wrong impression about You because we didn't understand the ways You speak to us today—because we saw You only as others taught us to see You. We pray the Holy Spirit will use this message to stir up, motivate, cleanse, and cultivate our lives. Use it, Father, to compel us to continue to seek You each day and listen for Your gentle voice.*

# Notes and Prayer Requests

Use this space to write any key points, questions, or prayer requests from this week's study.

# How God Has Spoken

## IN THIS LESSON

*Learning:* What are some of the ways that God speaks to people today?

*Growing:* How can I learn to recognize God's voice?

In the Scripture, we find that God has used a variety of ways to speak to His people throughout the ages. He apparently talked face to face on a daily basis with Adam "in the cool of the day" in the Garden of Eden (Genesis 3:8). However, after Adam and Eve sinned and were expelled from the Garden, the Lord had to turn to other forms of communication with His beloved creation.

As we look at the Scriptures, we find at least eight different ways in which God spoke to His people during biblical times: (1) direct revelations, (2) dreams, (3) written words, (4) prophets, (5) circumstances, (6) angels, (7) Jesus Christ, and (8) the Holy Spirit. We will explore each of these eight ways briefly in this lesson. However, before we begin, I want to indicate at the outset there are two ways in which God *did not* and *does not* speak to His people.

# WAYS GOD DOES
# NOT SPEAK TO PEOPLE

*First, God does not speak to His people through natural phenomena.* I realize that this statement may seem strange, as many of us say we feel closer to God when we are in the great outdoors. I am a lover of God's natural world, and few things delight me as much as seeing the beauty of nature. However, having feelings about God's presence and His creation is not the same as claiming we have a message from God through some act of nature.

For instance, we cannot observe a volcanic eruption or a hurricane and say, "Look at what God is saying." Neither can we perceive a pattern in the ashes of a fireplace and conclude, "This is God's word." I know a man who once saw a cross shape in the clouds as he was flying in a jet and concluded it was a sign that he was saved. A glint in the skies does not have anything to do with confessing our sinful state, receiving God's forgiveness, or believing in Jesus Christ and confessing Him as Savior and Lord, which is the pattern the Bible gives for our salvation.

The broad message of God in nature is that He is orderly and operates His universe according to a purpose, design, and intention. We see in nature that God loves beauty and provides amply for His children. Nature speaks of God. But this is far different from saying, "God speaks through nature with a personal word to us."

Now, we must be clear on this point so as not to misunderstand how God *may* use natural means to confirm His word to us or reveal His timing to us. For example, in 1 Kings 18 we read how Elijah received a message from God that a drought taking place in the land of Israel was about to end. Elijah told King Ahab, "Go up, eat and drink; for there is the sound of abundance of rain" (verse 41). After Elijah said these words, he sent his servant to the top of a mountain to look out toward the sea. On the seventh trip, the servant reported, "There is a cloud, as small as a man's hand, rising out of the sea!" Elijah perceived that God was fulfilling His word, and he sent a message to the king, "Prepare your chariot, and go down before the rain stops you" (verse 44).

Note that Elijah received the word of the Lord *first* and was looking for the fulfillment of that word. God used a natural phenomenon to confirm what Elijah had already heard. It's critical to see this difference. Many people make a grave error in assuming God is giving them a message when they see some twist of a twig or a breeze from a certain direction. When we try to see God's message in this manner, we are dangerously close to the practice of divination.

*Second, God does not speak to His people through occult practices.* God condemns the act of divination—the attempt to discern His message through things such as the pattern of tea leaves or the position of the stars. God does not speak through astrology or fortune-tellers, which the Bible calls abominations (see Acts 16:16–18). God speaks strongly against conjuring spirits (such as in séances) and any form of magic that might attempt to give us direction.

Soothsayers and seers were among the people whom God told His children to avoid (see Deuteronomy 18:10). We are to stay far away from such things as tarot cards, Ouija boards, crystals, magic charms, and other such paraphernalia associated with the occult. They are not methods God has ever used. Yet they are among the methods the enemy of our souls will use to try to deceive us into believing something that is wrong . . . deadly wrong.

1. "The heavens declare the glory of God; and the firmament shows His handiwork" (Psalm 19:1). The Bible shows that nature

speaks of God, but how is this far different from believing that God speaks through nature to you personally?

........................................................................................

........................................................................................

........................................................................................

........................................................................................

........................................................................................

**2.** "Give no regard to mediums and familiar spirits; do not seek after them, to be defiled by them" (Leviticus 19:31). What is the danger in trying to hear God through means such as tarot cards, mediums, and other practices associated with the occult?

........................................................................................

........................................................................................

........................................................................................

........................................................................................

........................................................................................

........................................................................................

## GOD SPEAKS THROUGH DIRECT REVELATION AND VISIONS

Now that we have examined some ways that God does *not* speak, we can look at some of the ways that He *does* speak to us. First, *God speaks through direct revelation*. This may be what many people today regard as an audible voice of God. It can also be thought of as a strong impression—one that comes unexpectedly, is absolutely clear, and is very specific.

Abraham had a direct revelation from God, who said to Him, "Get out of your country . . . to a land that I will show you" (Genesis 12:1). Moses also had a direct revelation from God when he was tending sheep and saw a bush "burning with fire, but the bush was not consumed" (Exodus 3:2). God saw Moses had turned aside to look, and knew He had Moses' attention, so He called to him from the midst of the bush. He gave Moses specific instructions to return to Egypt and bring the children of Israel out of slavery. Jesus apparently also enjoyed direct revelation from the Father in an ongoing way (see John 12:49–50).

*God also speaks through dreams and visions.* In the Bible, we read how Joseph had two notable dreams. In one he saw himself and his brothers binding sheaves in a field of wheat, and all of the sheaves bowed down to his sheaf. In the other dream, the sun, moon, and eleven stars bowed down to Joseph (see Genesis 37:5–10). Those were prophetic dreams about what was to happen later in Joseph's life.

Likewise, Daniel had visions in which God revealed to him the destiny of the world and the empires that were to come. Joseph, the husband of Mary, had two remarkable dreams—one in which he felt convinced he should take Mary to be his wife and the other in which he saw God's direction to take Mary and Jesus to Egypt. Peter had a vision that led to his sharing the gospel with the house of Cornelius, thereby extending the gospel to all Gentiles.

There are four items to recognize about dreams and visions as a source of God's word. First, dreams and visions that bear God's direct message are rare. Some dreams are of our own creation, and some are the result of the mind processing information. Second, not all dreams and visions are meant to be shared fully and freely with everybody in hearing range. Third, in no place in Scripture are we commanded to pray for dreams and visions or request God to give them to us. Dreams and visions are at God's initiative. Fourth, dreams are confirmed by outward circumstances. If God gives a dream or vision, it will ultimately come to pass!

**3.** "Now the LORD came and stood and called as at other times, 'Samuel! Samuel!' And Samuel answered, 'Speak, for Your servant hears'" (2 Samuel 3:10). What does Samuel's response say about how we should respond when we hear God's voice?

.......................................................................................

.......................................................................................

.......................................................................................

.......................................................................................

.......................................................................................

.......................................................................................

.......................................................................................

**4.** "While Peter thought about the vision, the Spirit said to him, 'Behold, three men are seeking you. Arise therefore, go down and go with them, doubting nothing; for I have sent them'" (Acts 10:19–20). How did Peter know the vision he received was from God? How did the Holy Spirit confirm the vision to him?

.......................................................................................

.......................................................................................

.......................................................................................

.......................................................................................

.......................................................................................

.......................................................................................

.......................................................................................

## GOD SPEAKS THROUGH THE WRITTEN WORD AND PROPHETS

*God speaks through the written Word.* In Exodus 31:18, we read, "When [God] had made an end of speaking with [Moses] on Mount Sinai, He gave Moses two tablets of the Testimony, tablets of stone, written with the finger of God." The Hebrews were among the first people to have an alphabet and record documents. The reading of the Torah, the first five books of the Old Testament, has been a mainstay in synagogue services through the centuries.

In New Testament times, the early church spread God's commands through spoken and written means. In fact, much of the New Testament was originally written as letters from the apostles to the various groups of believers throughout the Roman Empire. The believers also documented the ministry and teachings of Jesus in the Gospels. Behind the written Word of God is the inspiration of God. As Paul writes, "All Scripture is given by inspiration of God, and is profitable for doctrine, for reproof, for correction, for instruction in righteousness, that the man of God may be complete, thoroughly equipped for every good work" (2 Timothy 3:16–17).

*God also speaks through prophets.* In the Old Testament, we read how those who spoke the words of God felt they had little choice in the matter. The message they received was so overwhelming they could do nothing else but speak. Isaiah spoke of it as a "live coal" applied to his lips (Isaiah 6:6). Jeremiah described God's word as being "in my heart like a burning fire shut up in my bones" (Jeremiah 20:9).

The prophets did far more than foretell future events. In many ways, their words can be considered prophetic from the standpoint they spelled out what was wrong in the people's hearts. To be a prophet means to speak the truth of God to others. Sometimes, that truth is about trends or future conclusions. At other times, it is a specific truth about a particular circumstance. At still other times, it is the declaration of what God's Word says. God continues to speak through proclaimers today: preachers, teachers, evangelists, Bible study leaders, and others who proclaim the full story of God's truth.

Of course, we need to be careful in discerning who is telling us the truth. Our main source for discerning a true prophet from a false one is the Word of God. We must ask, "Is this person telling me only part of God's truth without any of the consequences for not heeding God's Word? Is this person telling me something other than what I can find in the Word of God?" If so, the person isn't God's prophet.

Also, what a prophet says comes to pass. If someone says God is going to do something and He doesn't—that person is a false prophet.

5. "The grass withers, the flower fades, but the word of our God stands forever" (Isaiah 40:8). What does this verse say about your ability to always and continually rely on the Bible as the source of God's direction for your life?

 

6. "Do not believe every spirit, but test the spirits, whether they are of God; because many false prophets have gone out into the world" (1 John 4:1). What does it mean to "test the spirits"? Why is it important to discern whether a prophecy is from God?

 

## GOD SPEAKS THROUGH CIRCUMSTANCES AND ANGELIC MESSENGERS

*God will sometimes speak through circumstances.* Often, the circumstances God uses to confirm His word will involve natural phenomena. One of the most notable examples is the story of Gideon, who was unsure he was hearing from God. Gideon asked the Lord to confirm His command to lead the people in battle by laying out a fleece and asking God to make it wet and the ground around it dry the following morning. Sure enough, the next morning the fleece was wet and the ground dry. Next, Gideon asked the fleece be dry in the midst of wet grass. Again, God gave Gideon the assurance he needed by doing as he asked (see Judges 6:36–40).

I never recommend a person stipulate to God the method He should use to confirm His word. We are not in a position to require God to do our bidding before we obey Him. Our position is to trust Him and take Him at His word—to obey and leave the consequences up to Him. I believe we can, however, ask God to confirm His word to us. We can regard many of the miracles in the Bible as God's use of circumstances to confirm the good news of the gospel. They underscore the mandates of God and provide a second witness that God has spoken.

*God also speaks to us through angels.* The word *angel* actually means "messenger from God." God spoke through an angel to the parents of Samson, to Mary, to Peter, and to a number of other people in the Bible. God sends angels at His will and for His purposes. These angels come to people uninvited, unannounced, and unexpected. In the Bible, we see they were usually so awesome in form their first words were, "Fear not!" They deliver their messages, which are always direct and specific, and then leave. They do not engage in small talk, develop a friendship with a human being, or give ongoing guidance and help.

Angels appear throughout Scripture, but in nearly all instances they appear to people who are isolated from a larger body of God-fearing people—to those who have no other means of hearing God's message. The Bible refers to angels as "ministering spirits" whom God sends to help us. But again, they come at God's choosing and on the authority of heaven. They do not appear when we think we need help but only when God chooses.

It is important to note that angels are not deceased human beings. Angels are of a different creative order. People do not become angels when they die and go to heaven. People are saints, and the Scriptures tell us that saints will one day rule over angels, though we presently have less power and wisdom than the angels possess. Angels are strictly the servants of God. We are children of the almighty heavenly Father.

**7.** "How shall we escape if we neglect so great a salvation, which at the first began to be spoken by the Lord, and was confirmed to us by those who heard Him, God also bearing witness both with signs and wonders, with various miracles, and gifts of the Holy Spirit, according to His own will?" (Hebrews 2:3–4). According to these verses in the book of Hebrews, what is God's purpose in sometimes using "signs and wonders"?

**8.** "Are [angels] not all ministering spirits sent forth to minister for those who will inherit salvation?" (Hebrews 1:14). According to this verse, what is the role of angels?

# GOD SPEAKS THROUGH JESUS AND THE HOLY SPIRIT

*God speaks to us through His Son.* Jesus is God's supreme Word to us—a Word that appeared in fleshly form on this earth. He embodies everything that God desires to say to us—and everything that we need to know about God's nature, about our own nature, and about the relationship that God desires us to have with Him and with each other. Jesus Christ is God's full expression of love, holiness, power, and relationship. As Jesus Himself said, He is "the way, the truth, and the life" (John 14:6).

If you have any doubt about what God wants you to do in a particular situation, just look to the life of Jesus. Do what He did. If you have any doubt about how to respond to a situation, just look to Jesus. Imitate Him. The only way in which you are not to be like Jesus is in dying as a sacrifice for the sins of the world. Jesus did that once—*definitively.* "For by one offering He has perfected forever those who are being sanctified" (Hebrews 10:14). You are no person's savior, for Jesus alone paid that price. However, you are called to take up your cross daily and follow the Lord (see Mark 8:34), pouring out the very essence of your life to bring others to Him.

God has spoken through the life of Jesus Christ. He is the perfect fulfillment of all God's laws and commandments. Jesus is the Word of God made flesh.

*Finally, God speaks to us through the work of the Holy Spirit.* We will discuss this further in the next lesson, but for now we should recognize that God speaks to each believer through His Holy Spirit. "Now the Lord is the Spirit; and where the Spirit of the Lord is, there is liberty" (2 Corinthians 3:17). What assurance that should give to us! We have direct and immediate access to God's opinion at all times. We have the full counsel of God available to us. We have His presence abiding within us to lead, guide, comfort, encourage, correct, and challenge us. The Holy Spirit is, indeed, "God with us."

**9.** "The Word became flesh and dwelt among us, and we beheld His glory, the glory as of the only begotten of the Father, full of grace and truth" (John 1:14). In what sense is Jesus the incarnation of God's Word? What are the implications of this truth?

**10.** "I will pray the Father, and He will give you another Helper, that He may abide with you forever—the Spirit of truth, whom the world cannot receive, because it neither sees Him nor knows Him; but you know Him, for He dwells with you and will be in you" (John 14:16-18). How did Jesus describe the work of the Holy Spirit? Why is it significant that the Holy Spirit—which the world cannot receive—dwells within the believer?

## TODAY AND TOMORROW

*Today:* The Lord used many means to speak to His followers in the Bible, and He still uses these means to speak today.

*Tomorrow:* I will ask the Lord to help me hear His voice and be open to receiving what He has to say to me.

# CLOSING PRAYER

*Lord, we choose to listen for Your voice and hear from You—the God of the Bible. Thank You for showing us the many ways You have spoken to Your followers in the past . . . and still continue to speak to them today. We see that You are our loving Father, intimate friend, patient teacher, gentle guide, generous provider, faithful supporter, and understanding counselor. Help us to ever listen for Your voice, comprehend what You are saying, and follow Your direction.*

# NOTES AND PRAYER REQUESTS

. . . . . . . . . . . . . . . . . . . . . . . . . . . . . . . . . . . . . . . . . . . . . .

Use this space to write any key points, questions, or prayer requests from this week's study.

# THE PRIMARY WAYS GOD SPEAKS TODAY

## IN THIS LESSON

*Learning:* What does it mean to listen to the voice of the Holy Spirit in my life?

*Growing:* How does God use others to speak to me?

In the last lesson, we explored eight ways in which God has spoken to men and women throughout the ages. We must never limit God in the methods that He uses to speak to us, but from my experience and observations, I believe there are three main ways that God use to speak to us today: (1) through His Word, (2) through His Holy Spirit, and (3) through other believers in Christ Jesus. Those who desire to hear from God and want to put themselves into the best position to hear from Him will pursue His message through these three methods. Through these means, God routinely, daily, and consistently speaks to all people who seek Him.

# LISTENING TO GOD THROUGH THE BIBLE

The Bible is the Word of God and is God's foremost way today of communicating with us. In the Bible we have the complete revelation of God. He doesn't need to add anything else to this book. Through the ages, the revelation of God was an unfolding truth by God about Himself, and in Jesus that truth was fulfilled. As Jesus said of Himself, He didn't come to change anything about the law or the commandments; rather, He came to show us by His life's example how to fully live out God's plan in our lives (see Matthew 5:17).

God's Word is for all people because it speaks to the basic human condition. The Bible addresses every emotion, human relationship dynamic, problem of the heart, aspect of the psyche, temptation or desire, heartache or joy, and issue of faith, love, or hope. In the Old Testament we have God's laws and commands, complete with examples of how God works in relationship to His own law and what happens when we obey or disobey that law. We have songs and poetry that tell us about the nature of God, the nature of people, and the nature of the relationship God desires with each of us. We have promises of God's presence.

In the New Testament we learn how God gave us His Son, Jesus Christ, to live out God's plan before us. He became our role model, mentor and, ultimately, our Savior and the door through which we enter eternal life. We see what happened to the first disciples as they received the promised Holy Spirit and began to live the very life of Christ Jesus in their society. We find teachings that show us how the Holy Spirit enables us to live a life that is pleasing to God. The Bible covers it all! Whenever we go to the Scriptures, God will speak to us directly, personally, intimately, and effectively.

1. "This Book of the Law shall not depart from your mouth, but you shall meditate in it day and night, that you may observe to do according to all that is written in it. For then you will make your way prosperous, and then you will have good success" (Joshua 1:8). What steps are required for us to find help from God's Word? What are the benefits?

......................................................................................................................

......................................................................................................................

......................................................................................................................

......................................................................................................................

2. "Have I not commanded you? Be strong and of good courage; do not be afraid, nor be dismayed, for the LORD your God is with you wherever you go" (verse 9). Why did the Lord suggest that strength and courage were required for Joshua to follow His Word?

......................................................................................................................

......................................................................................................................

......................................................................................................................

......................................................................................................................

## SEEKING ANSWERS IN GOD'S WORD

As you pray and seek God's guidance about a decision, you should do so boldly as you ask Him to give you His wisdom. In response, the Lord will often direct your mind to a particular passage of Scripture that you have encountered in your daily reading of the Bible. He will bring to your remembrance His truth on the matter.

If you do not hear from God about precisely where to turn, begin by reading the words of Jesus. As you read, you may become intrigued with a particular line of thought, or you may be drawn to a particular word or phrase. You may want to use a concordance at that point to discover other places in God's Word where that word or phrase is used. In many cases, I have found that God will not directly lead me to a passage that holds truth in a given circumstance. Rather, as I continue to read and study, God will lead me step-by-step to the information that He wants me to see with new spiritual insight.

Eventually, you will come to a passage in Scripture that is directly related to your concern. It may deal with your experience in a way that seems uncanny or very familiar to you. Or the passage may deal in principle. You may find the key concepts that speak to your need. As you pray and read, trust the Holy Spirit to quicken your spirit to His truth. You may feel this as a warmth inside, or you may feel a great sense of absoluteness about a particular verse. Sometimes, the words on the page of your Bible may seem to stand out to you as if they were written in bold headlines. Other times, you may not be able to get away from a particular passage. It comes repeatedly to your mind, and you can't seem to shake it from memory.

Do not limit your search of God's Word to times of crisis or need. Read His Word daily, for it is as you read daily that God directs you, challenges you, warns you, comforts you, and assures you. Reading the Bible on a daily basis is like preventive spiritual health care. How much better it is to divert a problem or to address a matter before it truly becomes an issue!

In your daily reading, God will refine you bit by bit, always transforming your thoughts and responses into those of Jesus. You will begin to store God's Word in your memory, almost as if you are making daily deposits in a bank, so the Holy Spirit can bring the words of Scripture to your mind. Don't fail to read God's Word daily. Go to the Bible as if it is eternal nourishment for your eternal soul. Jesus said, "Seek, and you will find" (Matthew 7:7).

**3.** "If any of you lacks wisdom, let him ask of God, who gives to all liberally and without reproach, and it will be given to him. But let him ask in faith, with no doubting, for he who doubts is like a wave of the sea driven and tossed by the wind" (James 1:5–6). Why does the Lord require you to have faith when you ask for wisdom? Why will having doubts prevent you from gaining His wisdom?

........................................................................................

........................................................................................

........................................................................................

........................................................................................

**4.** In what areas do you need wisdom this week? (Write those needs below, and then ask the Lord to give it to you.)

........................................................................................

........................................................................................

........................................................................................

........................................................................................

## LISTENING TO THE HOLY SPIRIT

As you walk in the Spirit daily, surrendered to His power, you have the right and privilege to expect anything you need to hear from God. You can claim His presence, direction, and guidance by faith. In the Lord's Prayer, we read how Jesus pointed to this daily reliance on the Holy Spirit: "Do not lead us into temptation, but deliver us from the evil one" (Matthew 6:13). I believe this is how the Holy Spirit will guide you. He says *no* to everything that will bring you harm—and thus delivers you from evil and temptation. He will also speak into your heart a *yes* to everything that will bring you blessings.

In the Old Testament, when men such as King David inquired of the Lord, the question was nearly always put in such a way the answer was *yes* or *no*. I find it is much easier to receive the direction of the Holy Spirit by asking for such yes-or-no counsel than to say in general terms, "What do You want me to do?" As you do, you will sense in your spirit His word of reply to you. Generally, it will be a sense of enthusiasm and eager desire marked with great joy and freedom, or it will be a sense of foreboding, danger, caution, or need for silence.

Specifically, the Bible teaches the Holy Spirit will guide you and give you God's advice in four main ways. *First, the Holy Spirit will remind you of what God has said and done for you in the past (including God's word to you in the Scriptures and through the life of Jesus).* Jesus told His disciples the Holy Spirit would testify of Him (see John 15:26–27). In other words, the Holy Spirit would remind the disciples of all Jesus said and did and of its appropriateness for their lives. So ask the Holy Spirit to remind you continually about what Jesus would say and do if He were walking in your shoes through your circumstances today.

*Second, the Holy Spirit will give you the words to say.* Jesus once warned His disciples that they would be brought before the magistrates and authorities because they were His followers. But He then encouraged them, explaining the Holy Spirit would teach them what to say in such moments of crisis or questioning. You should likewise breathe a prayer for the Holy Spirit to give you the words when you face difficult moments and don't know what to say. You can trust God to provide words for you just as surely as you can trust God to meet your other needs. At times, the Holy Spirit may even advise you to remain silent.

*Third, the Holy Spirit will give you direction about where to go.* In the book of Acts, we read how the apostle Paul was once on his way to Asia when the Holy Spirit spoke to him and prevented him from entering the region. "Now when they had gone through Phrygia and the region of Galatia, they were forbidden by the Holy Spirit to preach the word in Asia. After they had come to Mysia, they tried to go into Bithynia, but the Spirit did not permit them" (Acts 16:6–7). Instead, the Holy Spirit directed Paul to spread the gospel in Macedonia. You can likewise trust the Holy Spirit to point you in the correct direction.

*Fourth, the Holy Spirit will guide your prayer.* Paul wrote, "[The Holy Spirit] makes intercession for the saints according to the will of God"

(Romans 8:27). When you don't know how to pray, ask the Holy Spirit to pray for you and through you to the Father. This is how you can know you are always praying in God's will. Then wait in silence for Him to bring to your mind various aspects of a situation or of a person's need. You may be surprised at the things the Holy Spirit prompts you to pray—things you had never thought about before.

5. "Likewise the Spirit also helps in our weaknesses. For we do not know what we should pray for as we ought, but the Spirit Himself makes intercession for us with groanings which cannot be uttered" (Romans 8:26). When have you been in a situation where you didn't know what to say? Did you ask God to give you the right words? What happened?

6. When have you asked for guidance from the Holy Spirit in your life? How did you find that He guided your actions?

## LISTENING TO THE WORD THROUGH OTHER BELIEVERS

God will often use other people to speak to you. Some may be total strangers. Others may be friends or members of your immediate family. He will use pastors and teachers and Bible study group leaders. In my own life, I have been privileged to receive the wise counsel of many people of faith whom I admire and respect.

At one point, I felt impressed to call together several men to whom I could open my heart fully and share the deepest wounds of my life. The men heard me with love and compassion. I then said to them, "Whatever you tell me to do, I will do." They gave me counsel that was truly God's wisdom, and as they prayed for me, God broke into some of the secret areas of my heart and healed me in ways I hadn't even known were possible. I experienced God's love in a personal way and with such great warmth and approval that I have never been the same since. God used those men to speak truth to me and to be God's voice to me.

God will give you counsel through the words of other believers—and at times He may use them to give you words of admonition. You need to be open to these words as well, as sometimes these individuals will be able to see more clearly the mistakes you are about to make or have made. However, as you open yourself to hear God's word from other people, you need keep the following in mind:

- *Make sure the counsel is in total alignment with God's written Word.* God doesn't forget what He has already said. He doesn't contradict Himself. If a word is from God, it will be consistent with what He has already revealed through Scripture and through the life of His Son, Jesus Christ.

- *Make sure the person giving the counsel has no ulterior motive.* When you are confused, in pain, or in need, you are more subject to manipulation than at other times. So be certain the person who gives you the counsel doesn't want something from you and isn't trying to manipulate you for his or her own purposes. Make certain, also, the person turns all praise and thanksgiving toward the Lord Jesus.

- *Make sure the word does not include something that might harm another person.* God doesn't cause one of His children to be blessed or to prosper at the expense of another. He also doesn't move a person into a situation that will cause another person pain, loss, or suffering. If someone advises you to take action that will damage other people—their reputation, property, relationships, spiritual growth—don't take the advice. It is not godly counsel.

- *Make sure the word is for your ultimate and eternal good.* God does not deal in short-term gains with long-term disasters. He always speaks to you in a way that prepares you for eternity with Him. So if someone gives you advice that seems to bring a great immediate blessing but carries the risk of long-range detriment, refuse the advice. God's word is always consistent over time.

Remember that virtually all of us first came to believe in Christ Jesus because somebody else told us about Jesus. Few have a direct revelation from Jesus—most of us hear the Bible preached in a way that compels us to believe Jesus is the Messiah, or we hear a person's testimony of relationship with Him. The best thing we can do is tell others about what Jesus Christ did for us on the cross.

**7.** "Where there is no counsel, the people fall; but in the multitude of counselors there is safety" (Proverbs 11:14). What is the benefit of wise counselors who speak the truth into your life?

.......................................................................................

.......................................................................................

.......................................................................................

.......................................................................................

.......................................................................................

.......................................................................................

**8.** "Test all things; hold fast what is good" (1 Thessalonians 5:21). What are some ways that you have tested the counsel you have received from other believers in Christ?

.................................................................

.................................................................

.................................................................

.................................................................

# LISTENING TO TWO OR MORE WITNESSES

Look for God to confirm His Word. He may direct you to two or more passages of the Bible that convey the same meaning. He may cause you to hear a sermon or a Bible lesson that is right in line with what He has said to you in His Word. He may bring a total stranger across your path to speak a word that seems amazingly on target with the sermon you heard last week. He may use a friend to speak to you or direct you to a verse of Scripture. These multiple messages to you are part of God's assurance plan that He is the One who is speaking and that He wants you to get the message without question or doubt.

**9.** "One witness shall not rise against a man concerning any iniquity or any sin that he commits; by the mouth of two or three witnesses the matter shall be established" (Deuteronomy 19:15). Why did God require His people to have two witnesses when establishing a person's guilt? Why not just one witness to the event?

.................................................................

.................................................................

.................................................................

.................................................................

.................................................................

.................................................................

**10.** When are some times God confirmed a word to you through two or more witnesses? How did you discern the word was from God?

........................................................................

........................................................................

........................................................................

........................................................................

........................................................................

........................................................................

........................................................................

## TODAY AND TOMORROW

*Today:* God speaks to us today through His Word, the Holy Spirit, and the words of other believers.

*Tomorrow:* I will spend time this week in Bible reading and in prayer each day.

# CLOSING PRAYER

*Father, we ask You that teach us how to hear Your voice through Your Word, through the Holy Spirit that dwells within us as believers, and through the words of other believers. We pray that this truth will transform our lives and that we will share this truth with others. We pray that You will use us, Lord, to speak Your words into the lives of others. We want to bring people to You.*

# NOTES AND
# PRAYER REQUESTS

Use this space to write any key points, questions, or prayer requests from this week's study.

# HOW GOD GETS OUR ATTENTION

## IN THIS LESSON

*Learning:* What are some means that God uses to get my attention?

*Growing:* What purpose does God have for using these means in my life?

When you walk in the Spirit, alert to God, you will hear what He is saying to you as a natural part of your spiritual walk. This is the Christian life—living keenly responsive to the voice of God in whatever manner He may choose to speak to you. You can have your attention focused on a person, a chore, or an idea, but at the same time you are so tuned to God's voice that if He speaks, you immediately turn your attention to Him.

Unfortunately, there are also times when you may choose to do things your own way. As a result, you head in a direction that will bring you to disaster or disappointment. God is speaking, but you aren't listening. You aren't tuned in to Him. During these times, God may use unusual means to get your attention. Prominent among them are these four means: (1) a restless spirit, (2) an unsolicited word from another person, (3) unusual circumstances—both bad and good, and (4) unanswered prayers.

When you look back at your life, you can nearly always find times in which God got your attention through one of these methods. His prodding may have been profound or gentle, but regardless of the intensity of His wake-up call . . . you awoke! And once awake, you were more than willing to hear Him speaking to you.

As you begin this lesson, be aware that God uses these methods to get your attention, but they don't necessarily have a meaning in and of themselves. In other words, you should not conclude that because you have a restless spirit, you are on the right track or the wrong track. I have met people who concluded that if they had a certain amount of nervous energy about something, it must be right. I have also met people who automatically decided that if they felt agitated in their spirit, they were sinning.

A restless spirit is merely an attention-getter—it is the *message* that is important! Certainly, your conscience may prick you about a matter and cause you to feel upset in your spirit, but the upset feeling is not the message. Your conscience is based on your understanding of right and wrong, and that understanding is rightly based on the truth found in the Bible.

In a similar matter, treat unusual circumstances like a restless spirit. Great blessings in your life are not an automatic message that God is pleased with you. In fact, the message that follows from such an outpouring may not be that God is pleased but that He wants you to do something with the blessings. Likewise, you shouldn't see a tragedy as God's curse on your life. Rather, you should perceive it as an opportunity to come before God to hear what He has to say in the midst of your need.

In the matter of prayer, sometimes you may be so eager to hear the answer you want that you fail to hear God's answer. You may perceive in these cases that your prayer has gone unanswered. However, this perception is not accurate, and it can lead you to further question, "God, why am I not hearing from You?" Such questioning, when done in an honest and soul-searching manner, can lead you to the position where you *do* hear God's voice.

1. "I say then: Walk in the Spirit, and you shall not fulfill the lust of the flesh" (Galatians 5:16). What does it mean to "walk in the Spirit"? Why does this require you to be attuned to what God is saying as you go through your day?

2. Why is it important to recognize a restless spirit, an unsolicited word, unusual circumstances, and unanswered prayers as just "attention-getters" from God? What happens when you confuse these devices with the message God wants to give you?

## RESTLESSNESS OF SPIRIT

We find an excellent example of God using a restless spirit to get a person's attention in the book of Esther. King Ahasuerus had been duped by Haman, his prime minister. Haman hated all Jews—especially Queen Esther's relative, Mordecai—so he tricked the king into signing an edict for the annihilation of the entire Jewish race.

But after the king signed the proclamation, he could not sleep. In fact, the king had such a restless spirit that he "commanded [someone] to bring the book of the records of the chronicles; and they were read before the king" (Esther 6:1). The king discovered during that sleepless night that Mordecai had saved his life earlier by reporting an assassination plot, and he decided to honor Mordecai for his actions. By the end of the story, the plot against the Jews was uncovered, and Haman faced the gallows.

In my life, I have found that God frequently uses a persistent restlessness to direct me. When I look back over my ministry, I can see clearly that every time God moved me from one pastorate to another, He caused me to feel restless for several months beforehand. This restlessness drove me to seek God so that, when the time came, I was ready to hear Him.

A restless spirit is not merely a case of nerves. This type of restlessness originates in the deepest aspect of your being as part anticipation and part uneasiness. It persists over time. When you have this feeling, the best thing for you to do is to stop and ask the Lord what He is trying to say. Spend even more time in the Word and in prayer. Don't attempt to outrun the feeling or throw yourself into some activity just to keep busy and to keep your mind occupied. Do just the opposite. Consider a time of fasting (from food, activities, time, or a combination of these). Set aside a block of time—perhaps a weekend or even a week or two—to quiet yourself before the Lord so you can hear from Him clearly.

3. "In the day of my trouble I sought the Lord; my hand was stretched out in the night without ceasing; my soul refused to be comforted. I remembered God, and was troubled; I complained, and my spirit was overwhelmed" (Psalm 77:2–3). What is the

source of the psalmist's restless spirit in these verses? What is the result of his restlessness?

........................................................

........................................................

........................................................

........................................................

**4.** When have you experienced this kind of restlessness in your spirit? What did you find that God was attempting to communicate to you during that time?

........................................................

........................................................

........................................................

........................................................

# A WORD FROM OTHERS

None of us enjoy hearing a word of admonition from others. We may *say* that we appreciate receiving words of correction or warning, but the truth is that we generally feel uncomfortable when they come. We don't like to hear about sin or its consequences . . . especially if the person is talking about *our* sin.

In the Bible, we read how King David committed the sin of adultery with a woman named Bathsheba, and then subsequently sinned by committing murder against Uriah, her husband. After committing these acts, David apparently continued his reign without any visible evidence of having a guilty conscience (see 2 Samuel 11:1–26). But then we read, "The LORD sent Nathan [the prophet] to David. And he came to him, and said to him . . ." (2 Samuel 12:1). David desperately needed to hear what Nathan said to him—but it wasn't a pleasant experience for him.

Of course, not all messages from others are negative. One time, I remember receiving a word of encouragement from another person who was almost a stranger to me. I wasn't at all expecting the compliment or word of affirmation, but I desperately needed it at the time. The statement was not in response to anything I had done or said to the person—and the person's positive word was so specific and direct that it caught me off guard! When I asked God about it, He let me see that He cared so much about me that He used the other person to tell me so . . . in order to startle me into paying attention!

Sometimes, you may dismiss such compliments or words of appreciation. But remember that these words of blessing may also be God's way of getting your attention—to get you to see your true worth in His eyes. The person who cannot receive heartfelt thanks or affirming words often needs such positive edification. At the opposite end of the spectrum, the person who cannot take criticism or reproof is destined for failure.

In either case, you must be extremely careful that others do not lead you astray with their words. People can use flattery, or veiled threats, or even verses and passages in the Bible to get you to fulfill their desires or do their bidding—all in the name of God. So, again, when someone comes to you with a message from God, take a look at both the message and the messenger. Weigh what the person says, and then go to God's Word and ask the Lord to speak to you directly. Count the praise or admonition as only an attention-getter that causes you to seek God.

Sometimes, the message that comes to you will be one of information. You may be puzzled, frustrated, or worried by what you hear. At these times, turn to God. See what He desires to say to you about the situation, about whether you are to act, and, if so, in what way and when. This is what Nehemiah did when Hanani, one of his brethren, came from Judah with a report about the distress of the people in Jerusalem and about the broken-down state of Jerusalem's walls and gates (see Nehemiah 1:1–11).

The word you receive from someone may represent a need in God's kingdom, the plight of fellow believers, or a specific plea for help in extending the gospel. If your heart is touched by the matter, or if you can't seem to shake the message you have heard, take the matter before the Lord to hear what He has to say to you about ways in which you should become involved.

**5.** When is a time that someone came to you with a word from the Lord about your life? What did you do? What was the outcome?

.......................................................

.......................................................

.......................................................

.......................................................

**6.** "The way of a fool is right in his own eyes, but he who heeds counsel is wise" (Proverbs 12:15). What benefits have you received from heeding the wise counsel of others?

.......................................................

.......................................................

.......................................................

.......................................................

# UNUSUAL CIRCUMSTANCES

Your circumstances can open your heart to God and turn your attention toward Him. I have seen numerous examples in my ministry of illness, accidents, bankruptcies, divorces, and other times of trouble that have brought people to their knees and to a total reliance on Christ. Sometimes this has been for the first time in their lives, and sometimes this has been for a renewal of surrender and commitment. Often, these circumstances caused the individuals to question life and seek answers—which, in turn, led them toward their loving heavenly Father and gave Him a greater opportunity to speak to them.

When trouble strikes, your first response should thus never be, "Why, God?" or "Why me, God?" In most cases, there is no good answer to such questions. Rather, your first response should be, "God, what do You have to say to me in the midst of this?" He will speak.

Unusual circumstances can also come in the form of blessings—which is certainly the type of attention-getting method I enjoy the most! The apostle Paul described this form of blessing when he wrote, "Do you despise the riches of His goodness, forbearance, and long-suffering, not knowing that the goodness of God leads you to repentance?" (Romans 2:4). The blessings God brings may be spiritual or financial, or they may involve your home or vocation. God just seems to pile on the blessings, and if you are not careful, you may assume you have a right to use these blessings in any way you desire.

Instead, ask the Lord *why* He is blessing you so abundantly. He may well have a special plan for you to use these blessings for the furtherance of His kingdom. If you fail to be sensitive to this plan from God, you can miss an even greater blessing ahead!

**7.** "The Lord passed by, and a great and strong wind tore into the mountains and broke the rocks in pieces before the Lord . . . and after the wind an earthquake . . . and after the earthquake a fire . . . and after the fire a still small voice" (1 Kings 19:11–12). What circumstances did the Lord use to get Elijah's attention?

**8.** When has an unusual set of circumstances led you to seek God in a new way? What happened as a result?

# UNANSWERED PRAYER

When it seems God is answering all your prayers, it can be easy for you to become complacent and just start to "cruise" through life without paying close attention to what God desires to say. During such times, the Lord may allow you to encounter a particularly urgent need . . . and the heavens seem to be made of brass! The silence is uncomfortable. You feel a growing desperation to hear from God and have Him speak His words into your life. God has your full attention, to be sure!

In the Bible, we read of several legitimate reasons as to why God may not grant some of your requests. You may be asking for the wrong reasons (see James 4:3). You may be in disobedience or rebellion (see 1 John 3:22). You may be asking for something that is outside the will of God (see 5:14). Or you may be in a state of unforgiveness with another person (see Matthew 6:14–15). At such times, God will refuse to answer your prayers because He knows that if He does answer them, you will stray further off base.

In such cases, an answered prayer may also cause you to respond with personal pride and error in thinking that your prayers alone led to a miracle, a healing, a blessing, or another person's salvation. Peter taught that our relationships with others can influence our prayers. Husbands, he wrote, are to dwell with their wives "with understanding, giving honor to the wife, as to the weaker vessel, and as being heirs together of the grace of life, that your prayers may not be hindered" (1 Peter 3:7).

Keep in mind that what you call an unanswered prayer might be a *no*, a *not now*, or a *not until* answer. Each is a valid answer, though it may not be the one you desire! The Lord denied Paul's request to remove his thorn of the flesh, and He instead gave Paul a grace sufficient to help him face and overcome his problem (see 2 Corinthians 12:7–9). Not all prayer is answered with a *yes*. Sometimes *no* is the best answer for your situation.

Also keep in mind there is no such thing as an "accident" with God. He has a plan and purpose for you, and even when bad things happen, you can trust that He is continuing to work for your benefit. Your role is not to flail your arms against a tragedy but to lift your arms to God so He might reach down and lift you up, hold you close, and speak His words to you.

God may use one method to get your attention in one circumstance and a different method at another time. Or He may consistently use one method to get your attention to the point that whenever you feel restless or face unusual circumstances, you automatically say, "I wonder what God wants to say to me?" Don't try to second guess God. Just recognize that He is a creative God and will use many methods to reach you and guide you.

Also recognize that God will not use the same methods for all people in like circumstances. He knows exactly how to reach each person, and He will employ various methods to cause that person to stop and listen to what He is saying. He will not let you walk into an open manhole, spiritually speaking, without giving you clearly discernible danger signs. He never quits trying to guide you into His wonderful plans and purposes for your life!

**9.** When has it seemed to you that heaven was silent? In hindsight, was there a reason?

**10.** "We know that all things work together for good to those who love God, to those who are the called according to His purpose" (Romans 8:28). What are some ways that even *bad* things can become *good* in the life of a believer?

_____

_____

_____

_____

_____

## TODAY AND TOMORROW

*Today:* God uses all things—good and bad—to draw me closer to Him.

*Tomorrow:* I will ask the Lord this week to teach me how to recognize His attention-getters in my life.

## CLOSING PRAYER

*Lord, thank You for never giving up on us. Thank You for continually working to get our attention and calling us to the right path to take—the path that leads to Your blessings. We thank You for Your patience and forbearance when we choose to go our own way and do our own thing. Thank You for the gift of the Holy Spirit, who always correctly interprets what You have to say into our own spirit, so that we can be drawn back into fellowship with You.*

# NOTES AND
# PRAYER REQUESTS

Use this space to write any key points, questions, or prayer requests from this week's study.

# The Hallmarks of God's Messages to Us

## IN THIS LESSON

*Learning:* How can I know whether I am hearing God's voice?

*Growing:* Where will I find the strength to obey God's will?

Jesus said of those who follow Him, "My sheep hear My voice, and I know them, and they follow Me. And I give them eternal life, and they shall never perish; neither shall anyone snatch them out of My hand " (John 10:27–28). What a great statement of hope and comfort! We can *know* the voice of the Lord, and as we *follow* Him each day and do what He commands us to do, we will never perish nor ever be snatched out of His hand.

You may say, "But how can I be sure the voice I'm hearing is truly from God?" I believe there are five hallmarks of God's messages to us—a means of determining whether the voice we are hearing is truly the voice of God. If you have questions about whether a message is from God, I suggest you line it up against these criteria:

- The message must be consistent with the Word of God.
- The message will usually be in conflict with conventional human wisdom.
- The message will clash with fleshly gratification and basic human lusts.
- The message will challenge your faith to rise to a new level.
- The message will call for personal courage to do what the Lord has said.

As we begin our study, let me again point out that consistency with God's Word is *always* our primary recourse in determining the validity of a message we believe to be from God. God never contradicts Himself. What He has set forth as truth in the past is truth now. He has proclaimed, "My thoughts are not your thoughts, nor are your ways My ways.... For as the heavens are higher than the earth, so are My ways higher than your ways" (Isaiah 55:8–9).

God operates at a higher plane. His motives are always pure and loving. His ideals are the most noble of all. His holiness is absolute. What God says to us is never going to be what the world teaches. God doesn't stoop to our level—He calls us to rise to *His* level. His messages challenge us to live up to the high calling of a life in Christ Jesus, pursue wholeness, and seek the fullness of our potential in Him.

God also doesn't call us to become something He doesn't enable us to become. He doesn't ask us to do things He won't equip us to do. He doesn't hold out a goal that is impossible to reach. God's messages will challenge us to be the best we can be in Him and to open our lives to receive the best He has for us.

# CONSISTENCY WITH THE BIBLE

God will never tell you to engage in any activity that is inconsistent with Scripture. This is why you can be deceived if you neglect the Word of God and don't build it into your life. You won't be able to tell if a message is out of line with God's Word unless you *know* God's Word. So, if you are making a decision about a relationship, a business matter, a new direction in your life, or any major change, start your decision-making process in God's Word. Go to the Word of God and stay there until you see clearly what He says about the matter.

When you take the meaning of one verse in the Bible and add it to the meaning of another verse and add it to the meaning of yet other verses, you build a foundation of meaning. You understand far more clearly the full wisdom of God on a particular matter. You err when you come to God's Word with preconceived answers and predisposed attitudes and say, "I'm looking for proof that what I believe is right." You are in a far stronger position before the Lord when you come to His Word asking humbly and honestly, "Teach me Your ways, God, and show me what You want me to see," and then let the Word speak to you in its fullness.

1. "Be diligent to present yourself approved to God, a worker who does not need to be ashamed, rightly dividing the word of truth. But shun profane and idle babblings, for they will increase to more ungodliness" (2 Timothy 2:15-16). What does it mean to be "rightly dividing the word of truth"? How is this done?

**2.** What are some examples of the world's "profane and idle bab-blings"? How do such teachings lead to increasing ungodliness?

.......................................................................................

.......................................................................................

.......................................................................................

.......................................................................................

.......................................................................................

.......................................................................................

# CONFLICT WITH CONVENTIONAL WISDOM

God's wisdom is not the same as the world's wisdom. A person who has grown up in a godly home, attended church, and lived in a community that had a high percentage of God-fearing people might have a different understanding of human wisdom than a person who grew up in an ungodly atmosphere, never attended church, and lived in a sinful environment. The godly person who is surrounded with godly people may become a little naive about what the world is like and say, "Well, what I hear God saying to me is what I've heard all my life." That person needs to recognize he or she has been blessed and his or her situation is relatively rare.

In most cases, God's message stands in sharp contrast to what the world has to say on an issue. The world says that you are foolish to give to God, much less expect His blessing for doing so. God says to give a tithe to His storehouse and He will pour out a blessing on you (see Malachi 3:10-11). The world says you are a fool to allow an enemy to get to you twice. God says to turn the other cheek when your enemy strikes you, giving him the opportunity to strike you again (see Matthew 5:39). The world says everything is relative and truth is subject to conditions and interpretation. God says His Word is absolute and unchanging (see Malachi 3:6).

We must recognize that most of the world is moving in the wrong direction. Jesus taught, "Enter by the narrow gate; for wide is the gate and broad is the way that leads to destruction, and there are many who go in by it. Because narrow is the gate and difficult is the way which leads to life, and there are few who find it" (Matthew 7:13–14). When God speaks to us, He calls us to His way of thinking and seeing. In the New Testament, this mindset is called the mind of Christ. So ask yourself, "Would Jesus do this?" If not . . . don't do it.

3. "Let this mind be in you which was also in Christ Jesus, who, being in the form of God, did not consider it robbery to be equal with God, but made Himself of no reputation, taking the form of a bondservant, and coming in the likeness of men" (Philippians 2:5–7). What is the "mind" of Christ?

.......................................................................................
.......................................................................................
.......................................................................................
.......................................................................................
.......................................................................................
.......................................................................................

4. What are some of the attributes and teachings of Christ that run contrary to the wisdom of the world? When have you encountered resistance from others for choosing to follow Jesus' mindset?

.......................................................................................
.......................................................................................
.......................................................................................
.......................................................................................
.......................................................................................
.......................................................................................

# CLASH WITH FLESHLY LUSTS

We should recognize immediately that any counsel is not of God if it urges us to gratify the flesh without any thought to the consequences. God gives us messages that please the Spirit of God within us, not our lusts and sinful desires. In fact, in 1 John 2:16 we read that every person must battle the "lust of the flesh" (human appetites and sexual desires not in keeping with God's plan for marriage), the "lust of the eyes" (covetousness and greed for material goods), and the "pride of life" (the desire for power and status that exalt one over others).

We err when we dismiss these lusts as irrelevant to us as Christians. We overcome lusts and temptations by the power of the Holy Spirit, but we never become immune to human appetites, a desire for goods and wealth, or a longing for fame, power, or prestige. We are self-centered creatures and, whether we want it to be so or not, we are usually out for ourselves and our own interests. We must keep in mind that God's voice does not feed our self-centered natures but He calls us to righteousness, purity, and unselfish giving to others.

**5.** "Do not love the world or the things in the world. If anyone loves the world, the love of the Father is not in him. For all that is in the world—the lust of the flesh, the lust of the eyes, and the pride of life—is not of the Father but is of the world" (1 John 2:15–16). What does it mean to "love the world"? What is a sign that a person loves the world?

**6.** What are some practical examples of the "lust of the flesh"? Of the "lust of the eyes"? Of the "pride of life"?

.................................................................................

.................................................................................

.................................................................................

.................................................................................

.................................................................................

.................................................................................

.................................................................................

# CHALLENGE TO GROW IN FAITH

God has given a "measure of faith" to each of us, and our faith is to grow (see Romans 12:3). God desires for us to come to the point where we have great faith. In the Bible, we read how the disciples once awoke Jesus to still a storm on the Sea of Galilee, and He said to them, "Why are you so fearful? How is it that you have no faith?" (Mark 4:40). Jesus was basically asking them, "Why did you not use your faith in this situation?" Peter walked on the water and started to sink, and Jesus said to him, "O you of little faith, why did you doubt?" (Matthew 14:31). Jesus clearly expected His followers to have faith, to use it, and to grow in it.

We grow in faith when we hear from God, obey what He says to do, and then acknowledge God's faithfulness to His word in our lives. If we aren't hearing from God, it's virtually impossible for us to grow in faith. The same is true if we aren't obeying Him and if we aren't looking for the fulfillment of His word in us. We must recognize that a faith challenge requires consistency, endurance, perseverance, and watchfulness on our part.

Jesus once told a parable about a widow who went repeatedly to a judge for justice until he responded to her. Jesus pointed out that God was not like the callous judge. "And shall God not avenge His own elect who cry out day and night to Him, though He bears long with them? I tell you that He will avenge them speedily." Jesus then said this about our tendency to give up too soon in matters that call for our faith: "Nevertheless, when the Son of Man comes, will He really find faith on the earth?" (Luke 18:8). We must persevere in our believing once we have heard God speak to us and endure until we see the fulfillment of God's word.

7. "I say to you, if you have faith as a mustard seed, you will say to this mountain, 'Move from here to there,' and it will move; and nothing will be impossible for you" (Matthew 17:20). What does it mean to have "faith as a mustard seed"?

8. When have you asked for something in prayer that you didn't really believe would happen? When have you exercised genuine faith? What were the results?

## THE CALL TO HAVE COURAGE

Finally, a message from God will likely call you to have courage. If you are being asked to move against the tide of conventional wisdom and act in contradiction to your fleshly nature, you are going to feel you are taking a risk in obeying God's message. Any time you take a risk for God's purposes, you are going to need courage. Joshua understood this need. The Lord had challenged him with the mission of getting thousands of grumbling Israelites across the Jordan River so they might claim the land of promise as their own. Prior to their crossing the river, the Lord exhorted Joshua three times to have courage:

> Be strong and of good courage, for to this people you shall divide as an inheritance the land which I swore to their fathers to give them. Only be strong and very courageous, that you may observe to do according to all the law which Moses My servant commanded you; do not turn from it to the right hand or to the left, that you may prosper wherever you go. . . . Have I not commanded you? Be strong and of good courage; do not be afraid, nor be dismayed, for the LORD your God is with you wherever you go (Joshua 1:6–7, 9).

Take a close look at these verses. In the first verse, the Lord reminded Joshua of the promised blessing that lay before him. Likewise, keep in mind God's promises as you stand in faith, believing God to be true to His Word as you step out in obedience to His voice.

The second time the Lord admonished Joshua, He said, in essence, "Stay on track. Don't stray from My commandments and laws." As you obey the Lord, you must stay in the Word, stay in fellowship with other believers, stay in prayer, and listen keenly for God's voice.

The third time, God said, "Don't let yourself get scared or discouraged. Remember that I am with you." Fear and discouragement are subject to your will, and you can command them to leave you in the name of Jesus. The same goes for worry or feelings of frustration that you aren't seeing God's results as quickly as you would like. Remind yourself of what you heard God say, stay close to Him, and refuse to allow yourself to give in to fear or discouragement.

The good news is the Lord doesn't expect you to have courage your own. The Lord says that if you need courage, He will strengthen your heart (see Psalm 31:24). When God speaks to you, the fulfillment of His plans hinges to some degree on whether you respond with a courageous spirit. His voice leads you not into timid discipleship but into bold witness.

Keep in mind that nowhere in Scripture does God tell anyone to rush blindly into a decision. There may be times when you need to hear from God and act quickly, but God will never tell you to rush in without consulting Him about His timing. Believers often rush in because they fail to ask God about timing. They assume that when the Lord tells them to do something, He means *right now*, but that may not be the case. He may prompt you to wait for further instructions or to wait until certain conditions are fulfilled.

So take time to make certain you have truly heard from God and have heard Him clearly and precisely. Above all, make sure He is finished with all He has to say on a point before you rush off to obey Him. His message may include instructions about whom to contact, where to go, and how to proceed. Make sure you have all the directions, insights, and details He desires to give you. Subject the whole of God's message to the points discussed in this lesson.

**9.** "Watch, stand fast in the faith, be brave, be strong" (1 Corinthians 16:13). Why does the Bible frequently command followers of Christ to be brave and strong? In what ways are such attributes a matter of choice rather than something with which you are born?

**10.** "For God has not given us a spirit of fear, but of power and of love and of a sound mind" (2 Timothy 1:7). What does Paul mean by "a sound mind"? In what sense can you have an unsound mind when you don't wait for the Lord's instructions?

......................................................................................

......................................................................................

......................................................................................

......................................................................................

......................................................................................

......................................................................................

## TODAY AND TOMORROW

*Today:* God gives me the strength and the courage to obey everything He asks me to do.

*Tomorrow:* I will ask the Lord to fill me this week with His strength and courage.

# CLOSING PRAYER

*Heavenly Father, we thank You and praise You for being so good to us. How often we have been passive when we should have been bold listeners. We pray that the Holy Spirit, who is living within us, would remind us that You are God. We pray that we would continue to seek to know Your voice. And we pray that You would continue to help us see the hallmarks of Your messages to us so we know the direction we receive is from You on the path we should take.*

# NOTES AND
# PRAYER REQUESTS

Use this space to write any key points, questions, or prayer requests from this week's study.

# How to Tell if the Voice Is from God

## IN THIS LESSON

*Learning:* Does Satan try to imitate God's voice?

*Growing:* How can I distinguish between bad advice and good advice?

People often ask me, "When I listen for God to speak after I pray, I sometimes seem to hear two voices. How do I know if I'm hearing from God or from Satan?" This is a legitimate question, because we know from the Scripture that the enemy of our souls will also attempt to speak to us. We know from Jesus' temptation in the wilderness that Satan will try many tricks to convince us to listen to him instead of to God (see Matthew 4:1–11). The apostle Peter warned the devil is always on the prowl, seeking to instill fear and confusion (see

1 Peter 5:8). We must be on the alert to make certain we are hearing God's voice as we listen for His answer.

Jesus told His disciples He had to go to Jerusalem and suffer many things from the religious authorities. Eventually He would be killed, but He would be raised from death the third day. When Jesus said this, Peter took Him aside and told Him, "Far be it from You, Lord; this shall not happen to You!" (Matthew 16:22). As well-intentioned as Peter may have been, his words were not God's words—they were words that lined up with Satan's message. Jesus turned to Peter and rebuked him, saying, "Get behind Me, Satan! You are an offense to Me, for you are not mindful of the things of God, but the things of men" (verse 23).

Peter had been a follower of Jesus from the beginning of His earthly ministry, yet Jesus likened him to the arch-enemy. We need to recognize that sometimes Satan's voice comes to us not in our thoughts but through the words of other people, some of whom may seem to be well-intentioned. However, the Bible assures us there is a way to tell Satan's voice from that of our Lord. I believe we will hear these distinct differences in the messages:

| Satan Says . . . | The Lord Jesus Says . . . |
| --- | --- |
| Do what you want to do. | Consider the effects of your behavior on others. Lead a selfless and giving life. |
| Live for the moment. | Live with an eye to eternity. |
| Don't concern yourself with what others say. | Receive godly counsel. |
| You're as mature as you ever need to be. You're a grown up. | Continue to grow and mature and to become more and more like Christ. |

Certainly, the outcome is different when we follow Satan's voice rather than the Lord's. Satan's path always leads to loss, destruction, and death. The Lord's way always leads to abundant and eternal life (see John 10:10). Part of the difference in the outcome is in the way we feel about ourselves—the result of following Satan's dictates leads to frustration, dismay, and worry, while the result of following the Lord's message leads to inner peace. As we take a look at each of these concepts, keep in mind no one is immune to being deceived by Satan. We can never say we are fully immunized against Satan's assault on our minds.

## EFFECTS ON OTHER PEOPLE

God sees the beginning from the end, and He also sees all people and the full impact that what we say has on others. God will never ask us to exhibit harsh or crude behavior. He will never lead us to do anything that might hurt another person emotionally, spiritually, or materially. God always works for the good of all His people . . . not just a few.

Satan, on the other hand, just tells us what we want to hear. He tells us we shouldn't worry about the rippling effects of our lives on others. He tells us that people are an island unto themselves and we should do whatever we please.

If Abraham had weighed the ramifications of his dealings with Hagar, he would have no doubt resisted Sarah's pleas to produce a child with her maid (see Genesis 16–17; 21). Likewise, if David had considered the severity of God's discipline over his decision to number his subjects in Israel and Judah, he probably would have listened to Joab's advice to halt the project (see 1 Chronicles 21). If you feel the Lord is leading you in a particular direction, ask, "How will this affect people around me? Will anybody be hurt by what I am about to do or say?" These questions help you weed out Satan's influence and hear the message God desires to convey.

1. "See that no one renders evil for evil to anyone, but always pursue what is good both for yourselves and for all" (1 Thessalonians 5:15). When have you returned evil for evil? When have you returned love to someone who did you harm?

2. Why are you commanded to pursue what is good? How is this different from merely embracing what is good? Why must you actively pursue it?

## GOD IS NEVER IN A HURRY

There are many references in Scripture that mention the "fullness of time." God isn't in a hurry. He deals in eternal consequences and continually seeks the fulfillment of the full scope of His plan and purpose. On the other hand, Satan always encourages us to act immediately, because he knows we will reconsider if we back off and think long enough about most things. If we feel an overwhelming urge to act spontaneously, we're probably better off to pull in the reins. God is interested in having all the details in their proper places.

King Saul lost his throne because he acted hastily. The prophet Samuel had instructed him to wait at Gilgal for seven days, but when the prophet didn't arrive on the seventh day, Saul decided to take matters into his own hands. He prepared burnt offerings to invoke the Lord's favor, even though only priests were permitted to do so. Sure enough, Samuel arrived as soon as Saul had made the offerings. Saul offered lame excuses, but his rashness disqualified him from being king (see 1 Samuel 10:8; 13:8–14). Getting ahead of God is a terrible mistake, and the consequences are always severe.

On the other hand, Nehemiah patiently waited for God's timing. He sought the Lord with fasting and prayer for four months until the Persian king asked him why his appearance was downcast. Nehemiah explained his concern over the devastation of Jerusalem, and within days the king sent him to Jerusalem with full authority and the necessary supplies for a major rebuilding project (see Nehemiah 1:1–2:9). It isn't easy to wait patiently before the Lord until you are sure you have the fullness of His message. But how much more satisfying the results are when you know that you have heard God's entire message!

3. "My soul, wait silently for God alone, for my expectation is from Him. He only is my rock and my salvation" (Psalm 62:5–6). Why did the psalmist urge his soul to wait for God? What role does your will play in having patience?

4. Why did the psalmist tell himself to "wait silently"? What role does being silent before God—and listening for His voice—play in developing patience?

# TAKING ADVANTAGE
# OF WISE COUNSEL

The book of Proverbs has much to say about the value of wise counsel. In Proverbs 13:10 we read, "By pride comes nothing but strife, but with the well-advised is wisdom." In Proverbs 20:5 we read, "Counsel in the heart of man is like deep water, but a man of understanding will draw it out." We are to seek godly counsel and to hear from those who love the Lord and are grounded in His Word.

I never advocate that a person seek out professional counseling just for the sake of getting somebody's advice. The counseling may be more damaging than the original problem. When we seek counsel from others, we must seek out people who have no ulterior motive over our lives, are eager to hear from God (and eager for us to hear from God), base their opinions on the Word of God, and are eager for us to check their advice against the advice of the Bible. If your counselor doesn't have these three traits, find a new counselor!

5. "All of you be submissive to one another, and be clothed with humility, for 'God resists the proud, but gives grace to the humble.' Therefore humble yourselves under the mighty hand of God, that He may exalt you in due time" (1 Peter 5:5–6). What role does humility play in understanding God's will? How can pride hinder the good counsel you receive from others?

**6.** What does it mean to "be clothed with humility"? Practically speaking, how is this done?

.............................................................................................

.............................................................................................

.............................................................................................

.............................................................................................

.............................................................................................

.............................................................................................

.............................................................................................

# CONTINUALLY VALUE SPIRITUAL GROWTH

Rebellious teens often say to their parents, "Don't tell me what to do! I'm a grown-up!" This is the attitude that many of us have toward the voice of God. It is an attitude of pride, based on an assumption that we know as much about any given situation as God knows. In fact, nothing could be further from the truth.

Ultimately, God speaks to us in terms of our surrender to His desires. His messages to us aren't about what we want—as what we want is usually limited, self-centered, narrow-minded, and short-sighted. Rather, His messages are about what He wants *for us*—which is always eternal, loving, and calls us to a higher and better way. The Lord's messages are about our yielding to Him, taking up the cross and following Him, giving up our lives for others, bearing one another's burdens, encouraging and building up one another, and behaving in a way that causes others to walk in righteousness before the Lord.

Satan comes to us and tells us we are wise enough in our own understanding to make decisions. This has been the temptation to humankind ever since the Garden of Eden: *just eat of the fruit and you will be wise as gods.* In our day, the lie may be *just do your research,* or *just get this degree,* or *just take this seminar,* or *just follow common sense.* All of these may be good things to do, but we err if we put our trust solely in our own efforts and fail to get the wisdom of God. The result will be just as disastrous for us as it was for Adam and Eve. We find ourselves in trouble any time we assume we can make decisions totally on our own.

**7.** "We should no longer be children, tossed to and fro and carried about with every wind of doctrine, by the trickery of men, in the cunning craftiness of deceitful plotting, but, speaking the truth in love, may grow up in all things into Him who is the head—Christ" (Ephesians 4:14–15). What are some examples of ways the world is "tossed to and fro" by winds of false doctrine?

**8.** What is required for a Christian to avoid that childish tendency?

# IDENTIFYING GOD'S VOICE

The net result of hearing the voice of Satan will be a gnawing and nagging feeling of frustration in your spirit. For this reason, stop and take note if you believe you have heard from God but continue to experience uneasiness and questioning as you attempt to obey. You have not heard from God! God's voice brings about a deep calmness in the spirit. You may be challenged by what God says, but you will not have a sense of inner conflict, worry, or a troubled heart.

The peace that God gives to you is what the apostle Paul described as peace "which surpasses all understanding" (Philippians 4:7). This is an inner peace that comes with a settled heart and, regardless of the circumstances you are facing, is never shaken. When that sort of peace comes to you, you can know you've heard from God and feel confident it is His voice: "Let the peace of God rule in your hearts" (Colossians 3:15).

Some people have calloused consciences and don't seem to feel anything in the wake of making a bad decision. Not feeling anything is a bad state in which to find yourself! After you have attempted to hear from God and you have reached a decision about something in your life, you should either have an abiding sense of calm, purpose, and peace, or you should feel uneasy, dissatisfied, worried, or uncomfortable. Pay attention to this feeling that flows from your innermost being. It is a confirming sign that you have or have not heard from God.

Over time, you will grow in your ability to discern whether the voice you are hearing is that of the Lord. The same is true for the voice of any person with whom you have a relationship. As a child, I often heard my mother calling me to dinner. I didn't have to wonder for a split second whether the voice was that of my mother. I had grown up hearing it. A thousand mothers could have called my name, but I responded only to my mother's voice. Likewise, as you develop an ear to hear what God is saying to you, you will come to know His voice unequivocally and immediately. He is your Father, and He calls you by name.

9. "Be anxious for nothing, but in everything by prayer and supplication, with thanksgiving, let your requests be made known to God; and the peace of God, which surpasses all understanding, will guard your hearts and minds through Christ Jesus" (Philippians 4:6–7). What role does the conscious choices you make play in combating anxiety?

10. What does Paul mean when he says that the peace of God "surpasses all understanding"? How does the peace of God guard your heart and your mind?

## TODAY AND TOMORROW

*Today:* I can know that God od will never lead me to do anything that is against His Word.

*Tomorrow:* I will ask the Lord to make me aware of the promptings and schemes of the enemy.

# CLOSING PRAYER

*Lord, there are so many voices in the world today that compete for our attention, and we need to discern how to hear Your voice. We thank You for loving us so much that You do not allow us to continue following the wrong voices in our lives but lead us back to Your course and Your ways for us. Today, we pray that whenever we receive correction from You, we would look up to You and the immediate response in our spirit would be, "Yes, Lord."*

# NOTES AND
# PRAYER REQUESTS

Use this space to write any key points, questions, or prayer requests from this week's study.

# Our Predisposition to Hear

## IN THIS LESSON

*Learning:* What is God's character like?

*Growing:* How can I be sure that God will not reject me?

Have you ever tried to tell something to a person who didn't seem to understand you—no matter how many different ways you tried to tell him or her? It's as if the individual had a blockage of some kind or an aberration in his or her mental processing. This is often the way it is with us in prayer. We want God to speak to us, we want to hear His voice, and we want to follow His direction for our lives, but the signal doesn't seem to be getting through to us.

Whenever we have a conversation with God, we enter into it with some history. In fact, I believe what we hear from God will be determined, in part, by three things: (1) our prior relationship with Him, (2) our understanding about Him, and (3) our attitude toward Him. The truth is we simply *won't* hear from God if we have not previously established a relationship with Him, or if we have a faulty understanding of Him, or if we have the wrong attitude toward Him. In such instances the fault is not His . . . it is our ours!

You may feel you are being blamed in some way if you aren't able to discern God's voice or hear from Him clearly. But remember that blame is not at all the intention of this lesson. Rather, my hope is that you will recognize some of the roadblocks that may have been built into your spirit toward God, perhaps through faulty parenting, bad teaching, unexplained circumstances, or your own past rebellion. As you recognize these roadblocks, ask the Lord to dissolve them. Open yourself to His healing power. Ask Him to give you ears to hear.

**1.** What is some of the "history" that you tend to bring into your conversations with God? How do you think that has affected your ability to hear from Him?

**2.** "Call to Me, and I will answer you, and show you great and mighty things, which you do not know" (Jeremiah 33:3). What are some things that you want God to communicate to you today? What roadblocks might be getting in the way?

# Our History with God

Each of us has a history with God that began even before birth. God has ordained us to be on the earth and has a plan and a purpose for us—even though we may not have recognized it. The only message unbelievers will hear from God, however, is that they are sinners who need Jesus as their Savior. Until a person has received Jesus Christ as his or her personal Savior by faith, that person will not be able to hear God speak on any subject other than salvation.

When we receive Jesus Christ as our Savior, the Bible says we are born again. We are taken from the kingdom of darkness and placed into the kingdom of light. We become the children of God. Our salvation experience is the beginning of a two-way relationship with the Lord. God is not motivated to speak to any of us on the basis of our good deeds or our needs. He is motivated to speak to us because He has a relationship with us. For this reason, if we are having trouble hearing from God, we need to reevaluate our relationship with Him.

Once we have accepted Jesus Christ as our Savior, we must take a second step. Salvation establishes a relationship with God and settles the matter of our eternal security, but we must move on from salvation into identification with Jesus Christ. He becomes our Savior and also our Lord. That is, Christ's life is now our own, and our lives are now His. As the apostle Paul taught, "It is no longer I who live, but Christ lives in me" (Galatians 2:20).

In identifying with Christ, we take on the mindset that what happened to Jesus happened to us. He was crucified at Calvary; our fleshly life was crucified and our sins were nailed to the cross. Jesus was buried and raised; we were buried and raised to a newness of life that will be unending. "Do you not know that as many of us as were baptized into Christ Jesus were baptized into His death? Therefore we were buried with Him through baptism into death, that just as Christ was raised from the dead by the glory of the Father, even so we also should walk in newness of life" (Romans 6:3–4).

When we accept that Jesus has broken the power of sin over us, we are free to walk in the Spirit and to become the people God wants us to be. We no longer live for ourselves and on our own. We continually seek to live as Jesus would live and trust Him to enable us to do so.

The extent to which we identify with Jesus will determine, in part, what we hear God say to us. If we are content with the fact we are saved, we probably won't hear God speak to us. But if we are seeking continually to become more like Jesus, and truly making Him the Lord of our lives, we are going to be listening for God's counsel about how we can be more like Him. He will speak to us readily about sins we need to confess, relationships we need to make right, new behaviors and opinions we need to adopt, new activities we need to pursue, and new blessings that are ours for the accepting.

3. "I am the vine, you are the branches. He who abides in Me, and I in him, bears much fruit; for without Me you can do nothing" (John 15:5). What does it mean to abide in Christ? How is this accomplished in the life of a believer?

4. What fruit have you seen in your life since becoming a Christian? What fruit would you *like* to see in your life?

# GOD AS FATHER,
# FRIEND, AND TEACHER

What you hear from God is affected by how you understand His nature. Each of us is born with a mental grid system of opposites. We tend to categorize things we encounter as good or bad, plus or minus, helpful or harmful. Over time, this grid system gives us a perspective on life—what we might call our *worldview* or *mindset*—as we transfer some of our thinking from the past into new areas of experience. When it comes to your understanding of God, you will apply this grid system, based on your past experiences, and come to certain conclusions about Him.

Let's examine several ways this grid system might affect the conclusions you reach about God. First, you may view Him as either a *loving or demanding father.* Do you come before God expecting Him to accept you, love you unconditionally, and embrace you warmly? Or do you expect Him to ridicule you, put conditions on whether He will love you, reject you, or fail to acknowledge you as His child? The Bible tells us God's nature is love (see 1 John 4:8), and because of His love, He sent His only Son into the world that whoever believes on Him might have eternal life (see John 3:16). If you struggle perceiving God as a loving father, look up verses in a concordance that relate to His loving nature. Write them out. Memorize them. Develop a new grid system in your thinking.

Second, you may view God as either an *intimate or distant friend.* Do you come before the Father with freedom to say anything you like, trusting Him to understand you and not reject you? Or do you expect God to be like a bureaucrat who asks you to fill out your petitions in triplicate, take a seat in the corner, and wait until your turn is called? The Bible says God is "near to all who call upon Him" (Psalm 145:18). Jesus is a friend who "sticks closer than a brother" (Proverbs 18:24). He said to His followers they were His friends, not His servants (see John 15:15). If you struggle to regard the Lord as your intimate friend, read the Gospels and observe how closely Jesus lived in relationship with those who followed Him.

Third, you may view God as either a *patient or intolerant teacher.* Do you expect the Lord to teach you the error of your ways so you might improve? Or do you expect Him to give you a failing grade, drop you from life's course, and suspend you from His school? God is not a critical teacher who is always harping on your lack of spiritual understanding or waiting to punish you for a mistake. He is a patient, kind, loving teacher who draws you toward Himself and the way of righteousness. If you think of God only as a judge and not as a patient teacher, go again to the words of Jesus in the Gospels. Read what Jesus said. You will find good reason as to why His followers called Him their *rabbi*—their beloved teacher.

**5.** "For you did not receive the spirit of bondage again to fear, but you received the Spirit of adoption by whom we cry out, 'Abba, Father'" (Romans 8:15). How do you perceive God when you think of Him as your heavenly Father?

........................................................................................................

........................................................................................................

........................................................................................................

........................................................................................................

........................................................................................................

**6.** "No longer do I call you servants, for a servant does not know what his master is doing; but I have called you friends" (John 15:15). In what ways to do you see God as your friend? Is it comfortable or uncomfortable to view Him this way? Explain.

........................................................................................................

........................................................................................................

........................................................................................................

........................................................................................................

........................................................................................................

# GOD AS GUIDE, COUNSELOR, PROVIDER, AND SUSTAINER

In addition to viewing God as a loving father, intimate friend, and patient teacher, you may find your mental "grid system" leads you to make other conclusions about Him as it relates to His care and provision for you. *First, you may view God as either a gentle or angry guide.* Do you see God as One who disciplines you to get you back on track or One who punishes you in a fit of anger? Often, people with abusive parents will see God only as being harsh, unreasonable, and extreme in His discipline. But the truth is that God gives you rules to guide you in His way.

Think of what it would be like to be on a hike in a wilderness area with an experienced guide. You would do everything the guide asked you to do, because you would see your very survival and return to civilization at stake. If you mishandled the gear, wandered away from the group, or took a wrong path, you would want the guide to correct you quickly. You would follow his advice without question because you know he was speaking for your benefit. The same is true for God. He desires to keep you on His trail, using your resources and gear wisely, staying with other believers, so you might ultimately come into the fullness of His kingdom.

*Second, you may view God as either an understanding or insensitive counselor.* Do you have a feeling that God understands your concerns? Or do you think of Him as not knowing or not caring about your desires, temptations, or emotions? Jesus came to show us that God cares about *all* aspects of our humanity. He proves God understands how we feel and knows how difficult life can be. But God also knows we can overcome temptations and live a pure and righteous life. A good counselor helps clients attain greater health and wholeness. The Holy Spirit is just such a Counselor. He desires to bring us to wholeness by binding our wounds and giving us the strength to move forward. If you struggle with the concept that God is an understanding Counselor, I encourage you to look up many of the references in a concordance that relate to *compassion, mercy,* or *merciful*. The Lord does understand—and He cares.

*Third, you may view God as either a generous or reluctant provider.* Do you see the Lord delighting in you and generously pouring out the riches of His glory on your life? Or do you see Him as a stingy God who plays favorites and withholds what you deserve? The Bible states that God has infinite resources He wants to give to you—and He spells out in His Word exactly how you can receive them! In the story of the prodigal son (which, in my opinion, should be called the story of the loving father), we see the portrait of a God who is only too ready and willing to bless His children with wonderful things. Jesus assures us that God causes blessings to come into our lives in "good measure, pressed down, shaken together, and running over" (Luke 6:38). If you struggle with this understanding of God, read how He provided for the Israelites in the wilderness, I suggest that you read verses in the Bible are related to giving and receiving. Our God is a generous God!

*Finally, you may view God as either a faithful or inconsistent sustainer.* Do you come before God knowing that He is trustworthy, reliable, and consistent? Or do you question whether God will really be there for you in your hour of need? The Bible proclaims from cover to cover that God is on your team. He never abandons you. You can count on Him. Lamentations 3:22–23 assures us, "His compassions fail not. They are new every morning; Great is Your faithfulness." If you struggle with the concept of God's faithfulness, look up the words *faithful, faithfulness,* or *lovingkindness* in a concordance and read the references associated with His faithful nature. God is the same yesterday, today, and forever. His desire for us is constant. His presence is abiding and eternal.

**7.** "Trust in the LORD with all your heart, and lean not on your own understanding" (Proverbs 3:5). What does it mean to lean on your own understanding? How might this lead to a faulty understanding of God as your guide and counselor?

....................................................................................

....................................................................................

....................................................................................

....................................................................................

....................................................................................

**8.** "The LORD is my shepherd; I shall not want. He makes me to lie down in green pastures; He leads me beside the still waters. He restores my soul; He leads me in the paths of righteousness for His name's sake" (Psalm 23:1–3). How do you view God as your caring shepherd and provider? What challenges do you have in seeing God this way?

....................................................................................

....................................................................................

....................................................................................

....................................................................................

....................................................................................

....................................................................................

## OUR ATTITUDE TOWARD GOD

There are three overriding qualities we must have in our attitude as we approach God. *First, we must be submissive.* We must recognize we are finite and God is infinite. We must recognize we are created and He is the Creator. We must be willing to do what He says to do.

If we don't have this attitude toward God, we will want God to put His stamp of approval on our preconceived plans, or we will want God to tell us we have done the right thing . . . which may not be the case. If we have that attitude, we cannot hear the fullness of what God desires to say to us. We need to recognize our attitude is one of pride if we are approaching God certain of our success and sure of our decision-making abilities.

*Second, we must trust God.* If we don't intend to trust in Him, we will never listen fully to all the details He will give us about how to obey Him. It will be as if we are saying, "Lord, I'll hear what You have to say, but I don't believe You will be faithful to any of Your promises, trustworthy in helping me, or honest in Your appraisal." We must come before the Father convinced He is going to lead us in the right direction and will enable us to do all He asks.

*Third, we must come before God with a thankful heart.* The Scriptures tell us we are to enter His gates with thanksgiving (see Psalm 100:4). We come with an eye toward what God has done for us in the past, which enables us to receive what He has for us in the present and the future. We should look back over our lives and recount all the ways in which God has been good to us. This is something we can do regardless of how difficult our lives may have been. We must recognize that God is for us!

**9.** "Therefore submit to God. Resist the devil and he will flee from you. Draw near to God and He will draw near to you. Cleanse your hands, you sinners; and purify your hearts, you double-minded. Lament and mourn and weep! . . . Humble yourselves in the sight of the Lord, and He will lift you up" (James 4:7–10). Why are you commanded to humble yourself before God? Why is this important in your relationship with Him?

**10.** Why does James say God will draw near to you if you draw near to Him? Why is your inclination important in the relationship?

.................................................................

.................................................................

.................................................................

.................................................................

.................................................................

.................................................................

## TODAY AND TOMORROW

*Today:* God wants to be in an intimate relationship with me, and I can trust Him completely.

*Tomorrow:* I will spend time this week giving thanks for all God has done.

## CLOSING PRAYER

*Heavenly Father, we want to cultivate a listening heart and have a hunger within our souls to hear what You are saying. We want to have a spirit of submission and be obedient to Your will and purposes for our lives. Help us today to approach You with the correct understanding about Your nature and the correct attitude about Your love for us. Develop our relationship day by day as we choose to dwell in Your presence and listen for Your voice.*

# NOTES AND PRAYER REQUESTS

Use this space to write any key points, questions, or prayer requests from this week's study.

# HOW TO LISTEN ACTIVELY

## IN THIS LESSON

*Learning:* What's the difference between listening and actually hearing?

*Growing:* How can I learn to listen more actively to God's voice?

Samuel was one of the greatest prophets in the Old Testament. I don't believe it's a coincidence that his first assignment from God was to listen for His voice:

And the LORD called Samuel again the third time. So he arose and went to Eli, and said, "Here I am, for you did call me."

Then Eli perceived that the LORD had called the boy. Therefore Eli said to Samuel, "Go, lie down; and it shall be, if He calls you, that you must say, 'Speak, LORD, for Your servant hears.'" So Samuel went and lay down in his place.

Now the LORD came and stood and called as at other times, "Samuel! Samuel!"

And Samuel answered, "Speak, for Your servant hears" (1 Samuel 3:8–10).

This story of Samuel shows us that there is a difference between *active listening* and *passive hearing.* Hearing is something you do with your ears. If your hearing is normal, you can't help hearing sounds within a certain range. Listening, however, involves the mind—and we all know we can hear sounds without paying much attention to them. Genuine listening is active. It involves putting the mind in gear to hear everything that is said as if it has meaning to the listener. This is how God calls us to listen to Him: *actively.* He wants our undivided attention.

There are ten key ways that we listen actively: (1) expectantly, (2) quietly, (3) patiently, (4) confidently, (5) dependently, (6) openly, (7) attentively, (8) carefully, (9) submissively, and (10) reverently. We will examine each aspect in this lesson. As you read each one, I encourage you to think about your life. Ask at each step, "Do I do this? Is this the way I open myself to receive God's message?" You will likely feel a certain degree of conviction about one or more of these listening characteristics, as few of us actively listen for God's word to us at all times. Consider that area of weakness to be an area for growth.

## LISTENING EXPECTANTLY AND QUIETLY

If we are going to listen actively, we must come before the Lord *expectantly.* We must anticipate with eagerness His speaking to us—and believe the promise found throughout Scripture that God *will* speak to us. Our expectancy is based on the Lord's reliability—that we believe the Lord will do what He says that He will do. Our expectancy is also an indication of our faith. If we believe God's promises to us and rely on His faithfulness as our heavenly Father, we will expect Him to speak to us and act on our behalf. The stronger our faith, the greater our expectancy!

If we are to hear from God, we must also listen *quietly* and allow Him to do the talking. The Lord says to us, "Be still, and know that I am God" (Psalm 46:10). Too many of us think of prayer as a time of rattling off a list of requests and then going about the busyness of our lives. Quietness is essential to listening. We are going to have difficulty listening to the still small voice of God if we are too busy to sit in silence in His presence, if we are preoccupied with thoughts or concerns about the day, or if we have filled our minds all day long with carnal interference and aimless chatter.

You may find that late night or early morning is a time of solitude and quiet for you. A noonday walk in a park may be a time when you can quiet your soul before the Lord. Ask the Lord to reveal a time and place where you might turn off the cares and worries of the world for a while and just listen to Him.

1. "Those who wait on the LORD shall renew their strength; they shall mount up with wings like eagles, they shall run and not be weary, they shall walk and not faint" (Isaiah 40:31). What does it mean to "wait on the LORD"? What promise does this passage provide?

**2.** "My soul, wait silently for God alone, for my expectation is from Him. He only is my rock and my salvation; He is my defense; I shall not be moved" (Psalm 62:5-6). Why is silence important when you are waiting for God's answer? How can such quiet waiting bring strength and stability?

.............................................................................................

.............................................................................................

.............................................................................................

.............................................................................................

.............................................................................................

.............................................................................................

.............................................................................................

## Listening Patiently and Confidently

Active listening requires *patience*. The Lord does not always tell us things all at once or instantaneously. Sometimes He speaks part of His message to us at one time and part at another. Sometimes we hear a message from Him only after we have been waiting for a season of time. We want to say, "Lord, here's my order today. Please give me an answer before I get up off my knees. You have thirty seconds." But that isn't how God works. He is not at our beck and call. We may wait for God's answer for what seems to be a long time, but God has not forgotten. He is likely preparing us to hear His message. Let that process happen in your life.

Furthermore, as we listen to God, we must be *confident* we will hear what we need to hear. It may not always be what we want to hear, but we can trust God to tell us what we need to know so we can make decisions and change certain things in our lives for our ultimate good. I find that people sometimes listen for God with their hands clenched. They are afraid of what God will tell them. In part, this is because they are afraid they won't be able to do what God tells them to do, or they won't be able to live up to God's expectations.

But would a good parent tell a child, "Here's what I want you to do," and then not provide the child with information about how to do it? Certainly not. Neither will the Lord tell us to live, move, or act in a certain way and then not give us full instructions and sufficient information to carry out His directions. We must be confident the Lord is never setting us up for failure. He sets us up for success—success in His eyes . . . success for all eternity!

**3.** "Rest in the LORD, and wait patiently for Him; do not fret because of him who prospers in his way, because of the man who brings wicked schemes to pass" (Psalm 37:7). How is waiting patiently related to waiting silently? How does one reinforce the other?

**4.** "Commit your way to the LORD, trust also in Him, and He shall bring it to pass. He shall bring forth your righteousness as the light, and your justice as the noonday" (Psalm 37:5–6). According to these verses, in what is the psalmist placing his confidence? What gives him such confidence?

# LISTENING DEPENDENTLY AND OPENLY

Actively listening to God's voice requires our complete *dependence* on Him as His agenda for our lives. Have you ever heard the comment, "Do it as if your life depended on it"? This is the way we are to listen— because our lives *do* depend on our hearing.

Do you read your Bible as if it is the very food for your soul? Do you listen for God to tell you what to do with the awareness that if He *doesn't* tell you what to do, you really have nothing to do? This was the position of the prophets in the Old Testament. This was the position of Jesus in the New Testament. This was the position of the apostles as they attempted to do what Jesus had called them to do. This is the position that we as believers in Christ are also to take today. We must have no agenda other than God's agenda. We must have no schedule other than His schedule.

We must also come to God with hearts and minds *open* to receive what He chooses to give us. To listen openly means to be willing to hear God correct us as well as comfort us, to hear Him convict us as well as assure us, and to hear Him chastise us as well as praise us. We will not always hear what God has to say if we come to the Lord willing to hear only words of prosperity, blessing, and comfort.

Unfortunately, the more unwilling we are to hear words of correction, the greater our need for correction grows. So come before the Lord humbly and depend on the Holy Spirit to bring to your mind the areas of your life that need to be changed. Accept both the positive and the negative things the Lord says to you about yourself. Recognize His words of correction are for your good and are just as loving as His words of comfort.

The minute you say to the Lord, "I'll do anything *but* . . ." or "I'll go anywhere *but* . . ." you are no longer open. The minute you say, "I trust You in every area of my life *except* . . ." you are no longer open. The minute you say, "I don't believe that You would *ever* . . ." you are no longer open. Don't put limits on what God may say to you.

**5.** "For what man knows the things of a man except the spirit of the man which is in him? Even so no one knows the things of God except the Spirit of God. Now we have received, not the spirit of the world, but the Spirit who is from God, that we might know the things that have been freely given to us by God" (1 Corinthians 2:11–12). Why are we completely dependent on the Holy Spirit for understanding God's mind?

........................................................................................................

........................................................................................................

........................................................................................................

........................................................................................................

........................................................................................................

........................................................................................................

**6.** "All Scripture is given by inspiration of God, and is profitable for doctrine, for reproof, for correction, for instruction in righteousness, that the man of God may be complete, thoroughly equipped for every good work" (2 Timothy 3:16–17). What is the difference between *reproof* and *correction*? Why are these necessary if you want to be "thoroughly equipped" for the work God has for you?

........................................................................................................

........................................................................................................

........................................................................................................

........................................................................................................

........................................................................................................

........................................................................................................

## LISTENING ATTENTIVELY AND CAREFULLY

When I am preaching, I can always look out at the congregation and tell the people who are *attentively* listening for the Lord to speak to them. They often have a pad open and a pen poised to take notes. They are diligently looking for God's directions. To be attentive means literally to attend, or to pay attention, to each word. This is more than just expecting God to speak. It is listening to each word for all nuances of meaning and all aspects of the message that God is giving. When we truly listen attentively, we don't miss a thing!

To listen *carefully* means to listen for the Holy Spirit to confirm the word we are hearing is a genuine word from God. We must put everything we hear to that test. It must line up with the written Word of God. It must be in keeping with the full example of the life of Christ. It must be in harmony with the way God has spoken to His people through the ages. To listen with care means we care enough to evaluate every message against the fullness of God's truth.

7. "Beloved, do not believe every spirit, but test the spirits, whether they are of God; because many false prophets have gone out into the world. By this you know the Spirit of God: Every spirit that confesses that Jesus Christ has come in the flesh is of God, and every spirit that does not confess that Jesus Christ has come in the flesh is not of God" (1 John 4:1–3). What does it mean to "test the spirits"? How does a Christian do this?

   .................................................................................................
   .................................................................................................
   .................................................................................................
   .................................................................................................
   .................................................................................................

8. Why is it so important to test every message? How does this relate to listening attentively and carefully for God's voice?

   .................................................................................................
   .................................................................................................
   .................................................................................................
   .................................................................................................
   .................................................................................................
   .................................................................................................

# LISTENING SUBMISSIVELY AND REVERENTLY

To listen *submissively* to God's voice means we listen with the full intent of obeying. If we plan to obey what we hear, we will obviously take the care to understand. This includes understanding with whom we should work. The Lord rarely calls us to undertake projects totally on our own. Even when God calls us to reevaluate a certain aspect of our personal lives, He often directs us toward a person we can trust to be a wise counselor to us.

When Jesus went into the Garden of Gethsemane on the night that He would be betrayed, He was already fully committed to His Father's will. However, He struggled with the Father to determine whether there was another way to accomplish God's purpose. There will be times when we come to God, listen to Him, and grapple with what we hear. We may not be disobedient, but we may not understand how or why God is working in a certain way.

Being submissive does not mean you automatically lose all your other longings. They may be with you all your life. But in the end, submitting to God's word is the only way you will ever find genuine meaning and purpose in life. Only as you submit to God can you hear from Him clearly and be in a position where the Lord can do all He has promised to do. Don't let a spirit of rebellion impair your ability to listen.

Finally, it is important to listen *reverently.* A reverent heart stands in awe of God. What a privilege we have to hear from the God of the universe! When we listen reverently, we listen with wonder—first that God would speak to us, and then that God would invite us to be a part of His plans and purposes. You must never take God for granted and assume He exists for your pleasure and bidding. Rather, you exist to worship, serve, and be a friend to God.

Jesus said repeatedly to His disciples, "He who has ears to hear, let him hear!" (Matthew 11:15). All these aspects of active listening are ways in which you demonstrate you truly have these "ears to hear."

So make a personal declaration today that you will listen for God's voice *expectantly, quietly, patiently, confidently, dependently, openly, attentively,* and *carefully.*

9. "He went a little farther and fell on His face, and prayed, saying, 'O My Father, if it is possible, let this cup pass from Me; nevertheless, not as I will, but as You will'" (Matthew 26:39). How did Jesus demonstrate complete submission to God's will?

..................................................................................................

..................................................................................................

..................................................................................................

..................................................................................................

..................................................................................................

..................................................................................................

..................................................................................................

..................................................................................................

10. "At the name of Jesus every knee should bow, of those in heaven, and of those on earth, and of those under the earth, and that every tongue should confess that Jesus Christ is Lord, to the glory of God the Father" (Philippians 2:10–11). Do you enter God's presence with a sense of humility or with a sense of familiarity? Explain your response.

..................................................................................................

..................................................................................................

..................................................................................................

..................................................................................................

..................................................................................................

..................................................................................................

..................................................................................................

..................................................................................................

..................................................................................................

## TODAY AND TOMORROW

*Today:* The Lord calls me to be an active listener,
having ears to hear.

*Tomorrow:* I will review the ways I listen to God and work
on areas of listening that need improvement.

# CLOSING PRAYER

*Lord, it is beyond our comprehension why You choose to speak to folks like us—except when we consider that Jesus has made us worthy and valuable in Your eyes. We pray that we will be active rather than passive listeners when it comes to hearing Your voice. Heavenly Father, You are our perfect Shepherd, and we want to listen for Your words expectantly, quietly, patiently, confidently, dependently, openly, attentively, carefully, submissively, and reverently. Help us today to be open to receive the message You have for us with the right attitude of our hearts.*

# NOTES AND
# PRAYER REQUESTS

Use this space to write any key points, questions, or prayer requests
from this week's study.

# HEARING GOD THROUGH HIS WORD

*Learning:* How do I hear God's voice through the Bible?

*Growing:* What steps can I take to grow in reading, meditating, and studying the Scriptures?

Have you ever thought about the difference between merely *having* something and actually *handling* it? I'm talking about the difference between simply owning something—having access to it—and really knowing how to handle it and get the most out of it. For example, there are movie directors who make entire films using their phones. They record video on their phones and do all the editing and processing through different apps and software. Everything they need can be downloaded and accessed right in the palms of their hands—if they know how to make it work.

Now, I know lots of people who have nice phones, but I don't think many of them (or maybe *any* of them) could make a movie with just their phones. They own their devices—they have access to them. But they don't know how to fully handle them in order to get the most out of them. I think something similar happens today with believers in Christ. There are lots of Christians who own a copy of God's Word . . . usually many copies. But can they really *handle* those copies? Do they know how to make the most of those pages? To get everything out of the Scriptures?

Let me tell you now: if you really want to hear from God and listen to His voice, you need to know how to handle His Word. This is what we're going to explore in this lesson—three critical steps for getting the most out of our Bibles so that we can hear from God each day. These steps are: (1) read the Bible, (2) reflect on the Bible, and (3) study the Bible.

## READING THE BIBLE

When we talk about really handling the Scriptures, we need to start with Isaiah 55:9–11, which offers a beautiful picture from nature on how God intends His Word to work in His people:

> For as the heavens are higher than the earth,
> So are My ways higher than your ways,
> And My thoughts than your thoughts.
> For as the rain comes down, and the snow from heaven,
> And do not return there,
> But water the earth,
> And make it bring forth and bud,
> That it may give seed to the sower
> And bread to the eater,

So shall My word be that goes forth from My mouth;
It shall not return to Me void,
But it shall accomplish what I please,
And it shall prosper in the thing for which I sent it.

In these verses, Isaiah is reminding us the Scriptures were never meant to be passive. They are *active*. God communicated them to us for a purpose—not only to teach us something but also to accomplish something in our lives . . . to transform us. Now, the reality of whether that transformation takes place depends on us. Why? Because there's a difference between *having* something and knowing how to *handle* it.

When it comes to rightly handling God's Word in order to hear from Him, the first thing we need to do is *read* it. Now, there are two questions I hear most when it comes to reading the Bible. The first is this: "When should I read it?" And the second question is this: "How should I read it?" Let's tackle those two questions, because they are important.

*When should you read the Bible?* Daily. When Jesus offered His model prayer for His disciples, He said, "Give us this day our daily bread" (Matthew 6:11). He didn't say, "Give us on Sunday . . ." He didn't say, "Give me the bread of God's Word here and there . . ." No, He said this is *daily* bread—necessary for our daily nourishment as spiritual beings. As we have said, the time of day is not as important. You have to figure out when is the best time to really maximize the impact you receive from the Scriptures. But you do need to read the Bible daily.

Maybe you don't feel as if you need to read the Bible every day. Maybe you would like to build that habit, that discipline, but it seems more like a luxury than a necessity. If that's the case, I would recommend you go ahead and fast on the days you don't read God's Word. In other words, If you don't have time to read the Bible, you don't have time for physical nourishment. We're talking about the words of life! Read the Word of God every day.

Next, *how do you read the Bible?* The answer to this question is that you read it carefully. You read it prayerfully. You read it expectantly—as if you really are expecting God to say something to you. This is not just any old book! This is God's book. So you need to read it with the same respect and the same expectancy you would feel if you were having an actual conversation with the Creator of the universe—because that's exactly what's happening each time you engage His Word. Read the Bible reverently, and read it anticipating that God has something to say in your life.

Another question I often hear is, "How much of the Bible should I read?" My answer is that it is up to you. Many people choose to read through the Bible every year, which is wonderful. But let me ask this: Is the Bible getting in you and through you during that time? Are you allowing the Word to make an impact inside you? Reading the Bible quickly, or in big chunks, will give you a good idea of what it's about. But are you savoring the Scriptures? Are they accomplishing something in your life? If not, you may want to give a try with smaller portions. Read one chapter a day and see if a more concentrated amount results in greater transformation.

1. What specific promises does God communicate in Isaiah 55:9–11? How does God intend His Word to work in His people?

..................................................................................................................

..................................................................................................................

..................................................................................................................

..................................................................................................................

..................................................................................................................

..................................................................................................................

..................................................................................................................

2. "Our Father in heaven, hallowed by Your name. You kingdom come, Your will be done on earth as it is in heaven. Give us day by

day our daily bread" (Luke 11:2–3). Why is it important to treat the Bible as God's "daily bread" for your soul?

......................................................................

......................................................................

......................................................................

......................................................................

......................................................................

**3.** What are some words that would describe your experiences when it comes to reading the Bible? When have you been especially impacted by a passage of Scripture?

......................................................................

......................................................................

......................................................................

......................................................................

......................................................................

## REFLECTING ON THE BIBLE

The second step in correctly handling the Scriptures is to reflect on God's Word. If we want to find someone who understood both the value and the practice of reflecting on the Scriptures, we need look no further than King David. Here is what he wrote in Psalm 1:1–3:

Blessed is the man
Who walks not in the counsel of the ungodly,
Nor stands in the path of sinners,
Nor sits in the seat of the scornful;
But his delight is in the law of the LORD,
And in His law he meditates day and night.
He shall be like a tree

Planted by the rivers of water,
That brings forth its fruit in its season,
Whose leaf also shall not wither;
And whatever he does shall prosper.

David writes the person is blessed who delights in the law of the Lord and meditates on it day and night. But how do you do this? The Bible reveals four steps you can take to reflect on God's Word and take delight in it. These are important steps—and, in fact, you *need* to go through all four of them, as you will never truly hear from God in a meaningful way until you learn how to be still in His presence and focus on His Word.

*The first step is to review your past.* In his letter to the Philippians, the apostle Paul reflected on his past and wrote that if anyone had reason to take confidence in his good works and religious zeal for God, it was him. He had followed God's law from his earliest days, was of the distinguished tribe of Benjamin, was a Pharisee (a class of religious elite in Israel), and had achieved a high standard of righteousness—he could rightly claim to be "a Hebrew of the Hebrews." But Paul realized all these things were *rubbish*—the only thing that truly mattered was his faith in Christ (see Philippians 3:4–11).

One of the best ways to keep yourself humble before God is to remember where you came from. There is something wonderful about spending time with God each evening to reflect on your life and review the course of the day. There will be good things. There will also be things you would like to change—even things that you will likely need to confess to the Lord. "Lord, I shouldn't have said that. I should have done that." In short, reviewing the past will remind you of the tender care of God in your heart all day long and throughout your life.

*The second step is to reflect on who God is and what He has done.* When it comes to who God is, there's a lot on which to reflect. You can reflect on His greatness—He is the all-powerful Creator of the universe. You can reflect on His grace—though He is all-powerful, He is also all good, kind, gracious, and sensitive to your needs and desires. You can also reflect on God's goodness. Remember all the ways He has faithfully provided for you and carried you through the most difficult seasons. He is good.

*The third step is to remember God's promises.* It is a wonderful experience to read about God's promises in His Word. Why? Because if you pay attention, you will see God fulfilling those promises again and again. When you know God's Word, you can pray His promises—"Lord God, here's what You said." When those promises are fulfilled, they become a living reality and a living testament to Him in a way you could never begin to fathom on your own.

*The final step is to make a request of God.* In Luke 17:5, we read how Jesus' disciples said to the Lord, "Increase our faith!" When you reflect on God's Word, your faith rises, your perspective enlarges, and you find yourself making requests of God without any hesitation. This is because the more you reflect on God and His Word, the more you come to understand He can handle all your requests—and that He loves to bless His children.

4. "This Book of the Law shall not depart from your mouth, but you shall meditate in it day and night, that you may observe to do according to all that is written in it. For then you will make your way prosperous, and then you will have good success" (Joshua 1:8). How are you to meditate on God's Word? What are the benefits in doing so?

...................................................................................................

...................................................................................................

...................................................................................................

...................................................................................................

...................................................................................................

...................................................................................................

**5.** What are some ways you can review your past with God today? What attributes of God can reflect on during your time of prayer?

..........................................................................................................

..........................................................................................................

..........................................................................................................

..........................................................................................................

..........................................................................................................

**6.** "Therefore know that the LORD your God, He is God, the faithful God who keeps covenant and mercy for a thousand generations with those who love Him and keep His commandments" (Deuteronomy 7:9). What are some promises that God has fulfilled to you? How has He proven to be faithful to you?

..........................................................................................................

..........................................................................................................

..........................................................................................................

..........................................................................................................

..........................................................................................................

**7.** "Now this is the confidence that we have in Him, that if we ask anything according to His will, He hears us" (1 John 5:14). What are some requests that you want to make of God? What does it mean to ask "according to His will"?

..........................................................................................................

..........................................................................................................

..........................................................................................................

..........................................................................................................

..........................................................................................................

# STUDYING THE BIBLE

One of the main reasons people give me as to why they don't read their Bible is simply because they don't understand it. They have a hard time following it. This makes sense to a degree. The Bible was written during a completely different period in history, and it can be difficult to comprehend at times. So, given this, how can you start to understand the Bible?

As we've already mentioned, you begin by reading it and reflecting on it. Once you do this, you take the next step by studying it. You dig deeper if you truly want to hear from God. Note that this doesn't have to be complicated. Let's say somebody committed a wrong against you. You know you need to forgive that person . . . but it's difficult. So what do you do?

You might say, "God, what does Your Word say about forgiveness?" You then use a concordance to look up the word *forgive*, and you come to the passage on the Sermon on the Mount in of Matthew—and you learn exactly what Jesus said about forgiveness. Then you look up other verses and learn more—and your understanding grows. This is what it means to *study* the Bible. Before long, God will show you how to handle your unforgiving spirit. He will show you how to move forward in fellowship with the one who wronged you.

You can study specific words, you can study a chapter, and you can study an entire book of the Bible to learn what *theme* the author was stressing to his readers. For example, the theme of the book of Philippians is joy. The theme of the book of Colossians is the Lordship of Christ. The theme of the book of Galatians is the grace of Christ. The point is, you shouldn't read at a surface level when you engage the Bible. Meditate on it. Study the Word of God.

In addition, get tools to help you study, such as a Bible dictionary, a commentary, or a good concordance. One of the wonderful things to which we have access today is Bible software. There are also many Bible-based resources available online. With the click of a button, you can have access to an entire library of tools to help you study. We have more access to more information about the Bible than any generation of Christ-followers in the history of the church. So use it. Study God's Word if you want to hear His voice.

There is no book in the world like God's book. When you read it, when you reflect on it, and when you study it and apply it to your life, you become a living, walking treasure house. You become so wealthy in the things that matter. Money cannot buy the wealth you have access to through the Bible. Death can't take it away. It's eternal wealth. And you know what? You've got the bank right there in your hand.

8. "Be diligent to present yourself approved to God, a worker who does not need to be ashamed, rightly dividing the word of truth" (2 Timothy 2:15). Why is diligent study of God's Word necessary in the life of a believer?

9. What are some struggles you have encountered in the past when it comes to studying God's Word? What are some tools you can use to overcome those hurdles?

10. How have you seen God speak to you through His Word? What impact has the Bible made on your life as a believer in Christ?

## TODAY AND TOMORROW

*Today:* God is ready to speak to me through His Word.

*Tomorrow:* I will commit to read, meditate on, and study the Bible each day this week.

# CLOSING PRAYER

*Father, we love You and praise You and thank You for Your Word. We pray today that we will handle Your Word properly and allow Your message to sink deep into our hearts. Whatever stage we are in life—young people, college students, older adults—we pray we will read Your Word and know how to apply it to our situations. We remember that You told us to pray, "Give us this day our daily bread." We want to seek the nourishment of Your Word each day.*

# NOTES AND
# PRAYER REQUESTS

Use this space to write any key points, questions, or prayer requests from this week's study.

# FAILURE TO LISTEN TO GOD

## IN THIS LESSON

*Learning:* What happens when I don't listen to God?

*Growing:* How can I evaluate myself to make sure I'm hearing and obeying God's voice?

Throughout this study, we've learned how to prepare ourselves to hear from God. We've gained a better understanding of the ways in which God speaks and how He seeks to get our attention. We've explored how to differentiate between God's voice and the other voices that attempt to influence us each day. These are critical skills and practices for living the Christian life . . . and for living it well. There's very little we can do to produce spiritual growth and spiritual material that's more effective than listening to God.

But this begs a new question: *What if we fail to listen?* God speaks to us clearly, and He is faithful to communicate His plan and purposes. But what happens when we don't hear what He says—or when we don't really *listen* even if we do hear? This is what will explore in this lesson. We will begin by looking at Genesis 3:1–7, as this is the first place in Scripture—and probably the best place—to illustrate what happens when we fail to listen to God:

> Now the serpent was more cunning than any beast of the field which the LORD God had made. And he said to the woman, "Has God indeed said, 'You shall not eat of every tree of the garden'?"
>
> And the woman said to the serpent, "We may eat the fruit of the trees of the garden; but of the fruit of the tree which is in the midst of the garden, God has said, 'You shall not eat it, nor shall you touch it, lest you die.'"
>
> Then the serpent said to the woman, "You will not surely die. For God knows that in the day you eat of it your eyes will be opened, and you will be like God, knowing good and evil."
>
> So when the woman saw that the tree was good for food, that it was pleasant to the eyes, and a tree desirable to make one wise, she took of its fruit and ate. She also gave to her husband with her, and he ate. Then the eyes of both of them were opened, and they knew that they were naked; and they sewed fig leaves together and made themselves coverings.

This account represents the beginning of humanity's problem with sin—a problem that has continued throughout recorded history. Yet it's hard to get a full understanding of the story if we don't back up a few verses and look at Genesis 2:16–17, where we find that God said to Adam, "Of every tree of the garden you may freely eat; but of the tree of the knowledge of good and evil you shall not eat, for in the day that you eat of it you shall surely die." When you read those verses, it's obvious God spoke—and He spoke clearly. There was no room for misunderstanding. He said, "you shall not eat."

It's also obvious, when you read Genesis 3:1–7, that Adam and Eve failed to listen to what God said. They failed to obey. So, in this lesson, we will do some work to unpack what happened and how these events apply to our lives today. Specifically, we will explore four consequences of failing to listen to God: (1) we are easily deceived, (2) we make prideful decisions, (3) we blame others for our mistakes, and (4) we miss out on God's best for our lives.

**1.** How do we know from this story that God *clearly* spoke to Adam and Eve and that they *clearly* understood they were not to eat from the one tree in the Garden of Eden?

..................................................................

..................................................................

..................................................................

..................................................................

..................................................................

**2.** What can you learn about your enemy, the "serpent" or Satan, in these verses?

..................................................................

..................................................................

..................................................................

..................................................................

..................................................................

## WE ARE EASILY DECEIVED

Both Adam and Eve heard God's instructions, but when the serpent entered the Garden of Eden, it represented a new voice in their lives—a strange voice—that was different from God's voice. And both Adam and Eve chose to listen to it.

In a similar way, when we don't keep before us what God has said, we are going to listen to the wrong voices. Think about how many voices you hear in a given day—how many points of view that are continually bombarding your mind, heart, soul, and spirit. It's continual! You turn on the television, listen to the radio, read a magazine, go online . . . and the voices are there. They bombard you with so much that is vain, empty, erroneous, non-biblical, ungodly philosophy. So you have to choose: will you listen to it or not?

Adam and Eve listened to the wrong voice—and as a result they were deceived by the serpent. In Genesis 3:2–3, we read that Eve explained to the serpent how God had commanded them not to eat of the tree of the knowledge of good and evil. But to this the enemy replied, "You will not surely die. For God knows that in the day you eat of it your eyes will be opened, and you will be like God, knowing good and evil" (verses 4–5).

Notice how Satan twisted God's words. In Genesis 2:17, God had clearly said that if Adam and Eve ate of the tree, they would "surely die." Now Satan came along and said, "You will *not* surely die." He used almost the same language, but with one little twist—one little deception that changed everything. Jesus would later say of the Pharisees, "You are of your father the devil, and the desires of your father you want to do. He was a murderer from the beginning, and does not stand in the truth, because there is no truth in him" (John 8:44).

Satan is a deceiver. He always comes to us with what he knows will appeal to us—to our flesh. He doesn't come to us with the truth. In fact, he cannot tell the truth because he is by nature a liar. But when we are not in the Word of God, and when we don't refresh our hearts and our minds with what God says, we begin to listen to Satan's voice. We open ourselves up to deception. This is when Satan says, "You need this . . . you deserve that . . . this is exactly what you've been looking for." When we listen to the enemy, we soon get into trouble.

**3.** "The fear of the LORD is the beginning of knowledge, but fools despise wisdom and instruction" (Proverbs 1:7). How does "the fear of the LORD" and listening to His voice lead to wisdom? How does listening to the enemy lead to being deceived?

.................................................................

.................................................................

.................................................................

.................................................................

.................................................................

**4.** Why is it critical to listen to God and *recall* what He said when you are facing a decision?

.................................................................

.................................................................

.................................................................

.................................................................

.................................................................

.................................................................

## WE MAKE DECISIONS BASED ON PRIDE

When we fail to listen to God, what we are essentially doing is expressing pride. What we are saying is that we can handle things pretty well ourselves. Eve had heard exactly what God said, yet she decided that instead of listening to God, she was going to listen to Satan. Satan had said that if she ate the fruit that God had forbidden, she would be like God. She wouldn't really die. She would be wise. She would understand the same things that God understood.

"So when the woman saw that the tree was good for food, that it was pleasant to the eyes, and a tree desirable to make one wise, she took of its fruit and ate" (Genesis 3:6). Eve listened to the voice of

Satan and decided to follow his advice. This was an act of independence on her part and an act of pride. She felt that she could find a better way than God's way.

The truth is that all our sin ultimately has its root in pride. In spite of what God has communicated in our hearts and through His Word, somehow we say, "I think there may be a better way." When we do this, what we're implying is that we know better than God. Let me say it again: *we think we know better than an all-knowing, all-seeing, all-powerful God.* That is pride in a nutshell . . . and it will harm us every time. It's rebellion in our hearts against God.

Once we give in to our pride, we start to make decisions based on whatever appeals to our flesh. In the Garden of Eden, Satan appealed to three facets of human experience—three facets of human desire. First, Eve thought about her *appetite* when she saw "the tree was good for food." Second, Eve saw the fruit was attractive, "that it was pleasant to the eyes." This appealed to her desire for *beauty*. Third, Eve believed eating the fruit would "make one wise," which means it appealed to her desire for *wisdom*.

Notice also that once Eve decided to eat, she gave some of the fruit "to her husband with her." Sometimes we get the impression that Eve was deceived while Adam was out doing something holy or spiritual. No, Adam was right there with her. They were both deceived, partly because they both made decisions based on their fleshly appetites.

Now, there is nothing wrong with our God-given appetites. There is nothing inherently wrong with desiring beauty or desiring wisdom. God is the One who gave us all the appetites we possess. He gave them to us—and He offered the Holy Spirit to help us keep those appetites under control and in balance. But we lose that control when we stop listening to Him.

**5.** "Pride goes before destruction, and a haughty spirit before a fall" (Proverbs 16:18). When was a time you thought you found a better way than God's way? What happened as a result of following that course?

.................................................................................................

.................................................................................................

.................................................................................................

.................................................................................................

**6.** "Therefore put to death your members which are on the earth: fornication, uncleanness, passion, evil desire, and covetousness, which is idolatry" (Colossians 3:5). What are some ways the world targets and tempts believers in Christ through their appetites? How do we put these things "to death" as Paul advises?

.................................................................................................

.................................................................................................

.................................................................................................

.................................................................................................

.................................................................................................

## WE BLAME OTHERS FOR OUR MISTAKES

When we fail to listen to God, we start making excuses for our mistakes. Typically, those excuses involve blaming others when everything goes wrong. In Genesis 3:8, we read that Adam and Eve "heard the sound of the LORD God walking in the garden in the cool of the day." Just imagine that for a moment. What would it sound like to have holiness, omnipotence, sovereignty, love, justice, righteousness, goodness, and gentleness walking toward you?

Previously, Adam and Eve had welcomed God's presence. But now that their eyes had been opened to the reality of their own sinfulness, the sound of the Lord coming toward them was terrifying. So they hid, because they were afraid. God quickly found them and then confronted them about their decision not to listen to Him:

> [God] said, "Who told you that you were naked? Have you eaten from the tree of which I commanded you that you should not eat?"
>
> Then the man said, "The woman whom You gave to be with me, she gave me of the tree, and I ate."
>
> And the LORD God said to the woman, "What is this you have done?"
>
> The woman said, "The serpent deceived me, and I ate" (verses 11–13).

Notice that when God asked if they had disobeyed Him, Adam blamed Eve, and then Eve blamed the serpent. How often today do we do the same thing—blame others for our mistakes? We do it all the time. We try to pass the buck for our own sinful choices. But the reality is we are always responsible to God . . . and that our sin carries consequences.

For Adam and Eve, those consequences were bound up in a series of curses, all of which we are still burdened by today (see verses 16–19). As a result of sin, our world has been corrupted. Our relationships have been damaged. Our physical bodies experience pain and death. Our days are filled with toil. We suffered a separation from our heavenly Father.

But there's an interesting element at the end of the story that we shouldn't miss: "Also for Adam and his wife the LORD God made tunics of skin, and clothed them" (verse 21). Remember that Adam and Eve were naked and afraid—which was one of the consequences of failing to listen to God. So what did God do? He killed an animal, a sacrifice, in order to provide for His children. Which means right there, next to the story of the Fall, is a picture of God's grace.

**7.** "He who covers his sins will not prosper, but whoever confesses and forsakes them will have mercy" (Proverbs 28:13). Why is it critical to admit our mistakes when we make them? Why is this often so difficult for us to do?

........................................................................

........................................................................

........................................................................

........................................................................

........................................................................

**8.** "Do not be deceived, God is not mocked; for whatever a man sows, that he will also reap" (Galatians 6:7). How you seen this principle of "sowing and reaping" in your life?

........................................................................

........................................................................

........................................................................

........................................................................

........................................................................

## WE MISS OUT ON GOD'S BEST

Adam and Eve's act of disobedience brought not only negative consequences for themselves but also for the members of their family. This is always the case with sin. Our rebellious actions always cause a great ripple effect of suffering and pain in the lives of those we love.

We've already seen how Adam and Eve caused suffering to each other. But things get worse when we move to Genesis 4 and read the story of Cain and Abel. In particular, the story of Cain murdering his brother, Abel, because of jealousy and pride. And it doesn't stop there. Cain was driven away from his family and forced to start a new life with another curse on his head. Cain's descendants continued in his violence and expanded on his bloodshed. The history of human civilization shows this cycle of suffering and causing others to suffer.

Sin isn't something we can isolate. It spreads. It multiplies. It always gets loose when we fail to listen to God. And it always leads to suffering and causing us to miss out on God's best. We miss out on His plans and purposes—which are always much better than whatever we come up with on our own. For Adam and Eve, they missed out on the Garden of Eden. They missed out on the perfect, sinless, eternal bliss God had planned for them from the beginning of Creation. The same is true for you and me on this side of eternity.

Don't miss out today on God's best for your life. If you want to avoid the consequences of disobedience—of failing to listen to God—you need to get into the Word of God. You need to get into a church that teaches the Word of God. As you do, you will not only learn how to listen to Him, but you will receive blessing upon blessing and grace upon grace.

**9.** "God is able to make all grace abound toward you, that you, always having all sufficiency in all things, may have an abundance for every good work" (2 Corinthians 9:8). What are some of the ways that you have seen God extend His grace to you personally How can you—by listening for God's voice and for His direction—extend God's grace to others?

**10.** How would you describe God's plans and purposes for your life? How do you see obedience to God's will as part of achieving those plans and purposes?

......................................................................................................

......................................................................................................

......................................................................................................

......................................................................................................

......................................................................................................

......................................................................................................

## TODAY AND TOMORROW

*Today:* There are always consequences when I fail to heed God's voice.

*Tomorrow:* I will take whatever steps are necessary this week to avoid the consequences of sin in my life.

# CLOSING PRAYER

*Heavenly Father, we love You and praise You for Your incredible provision for us. We thank You for the story of Adam and Eve in the Bible. Even though we know it is a narrative of tragedy, it is also an account of triumph. For even back in the Garden of Eden—at the outset of humanity's sin, disobedience, and rebellion against their Creator—You promised a Messiah would come and gave us a hint of Your redemption through the shed blood of Christ. We love You and praise You for sending Jesus.*

# NOTES AND
# PRAYER REQUESTS

Use this space to write any key points, questions, or prayer requests from this week's study.

# SITTING IN GOD'S PRESENCE

---

## IN THIS LESSON

*Learning:* How can I put all these theories into practice?

*Growing:* How can I learn to listen to God?

---

In this final lesson, we will put together the concepts we have covered in this study and look at a process of learning how to hear from God called *meditation*. In recent years, meditation has been associated largely with Eastern religions, but we need to remember that Christians have practiced godly Bible-centered meditation for centuries. You may be more comfortable using the term *reflection* or *contemplation*. I like the phrase, "sitting before the Lord."

When King David began making plans to build a temple for the Lord in Jerusalem, the Bible states he "went in and sat before the

Lord" (2 Samuel 7:18). This is a descriptive phrase to me—one that defines our spiritual demeanor more than our physical posture. The usual position for Jewish prayer was to stand in God's presence. But David was sitting, kneeling, and resting back on his heels, humbly listening for what God was going to say to him.

When it comes to "sitting before the Lord" and spending time in meditation, there are five basic steps we need to follow: (1) set aside time, (2) get still before the Lord, (3) recall the Lord's goodness, (4) make a request, and (5) submit our will to God's answer. As we discuss each step, I encourage you to think, "How can I do this?" It isn't enough to learn these steps. You need to do them and have an experience of listening to God and hearing from Him.

After we go through the steps of meditation, we will turn to the results that virtually all people experience after a time of meditation. These include an abiding sense of inner peace, a renewal of a positive attitude, a feeling of personal intimacy with the Lord, an inner realization of purification, and a passion to obey God in the future.

1. "The Lord is good to those who wait for Him, to the soul who seeks Him" (Lamentations 3:25). What does it mean to wait on the Lord? In what ways to do you seek the Lord?

**2.** "I will meditate on Your precepts, and contemplate Your ways. I will delight myself in Your statutes; I will not forget Your word" (Psalm 119:15-16). Why is it important to meditate on God's precepts and contemplate His ways if you want to hear His voice?

........................................................................................

........................................................................................

........................................................................................

........................................................................................

........................................................................................

........................................................................................

# SETTING ASIDE TIME WITH GOD

Meditation requires a commitment of time. I encourage you to think of this as a *season* of time. The exact length of time, whether five minutes or an hour, will be determined by your purpose and your state of being as you come before the Lord. If you are in deep distress or if you face a major decision in your life, you should count on spending a longer time with the Lord.

Discuss your need to be alone with the Lord with your family members and others who depend on you. Find a time and place where you can be exclusively with Him. Make an appointment with the Lord. I sometimes go away for a weekend or an entire week to be alone with God. At other times I designate a half day to do nothing but sit in God's presence with my Bible open before me. Set aside enough time to go through the process of slowing down. Note that it can take a while to turn your full attention away from the cares of the world.

In anticipation of your time with the Lord, ask God to do the following three things in your life. *First, pray that you will have an open mind and heart.* Don't come into a time of meditation before the Lord with a closed spirit. *Second, pray that God will help you to have a clear mind and heart.* Your desire must be to hear the voice of God and have a firm understanding that what you hear is in line with God's Word. Ask the Lord to remove any doubt or vacillation from your thinking. *Finally, pray that the Lord will help you have an uncluttered mind and heart.* Ask God to help you put aside the worries, frustrations, and concerns you have.

Ask the Lord to help you stay focused on Him during your meditation time. Remember that your goal in coming before the Lord is to have a mind committed to hearing from Him, not to have a closed, cloudy, or cluttered mind. So ask the Lord to help you in this regard so your meditation time will bear good fruit. The feelings associated with setting aside time are usually eagerness, anticipation, focus, self-control, purpose, and a hunger to hear from God.

3. How easy or difficult do you find it to set aside time to be with God each day? What challenges and obstacles do you typically face in carving out this time?

4. What were your feelings as you anticipated your appointment with God? (Record them below after your time of meditation.)

# GETTING STILL BEFORE GOD AND RECALLING HIS GOODNESS

As you begin your time of meditation, get still before God. Fix your thoughts on Him. True stillness before the Lord involves a sense of relaxation and ease in the Lord's presence. I find the most wonderful stillness comes when I see Him as friend, walking and talking with me along the beach or mountain trail, or sitting beside me in my living room or study, or sitting opposite me at the kitchen table. The Lord desires to be with you. The feelings often associated with stillness are awe, wonder, awareness, closeness, ease, delight, and timelessness.

Next, recall the goodness of God. Many times in the Old Testament, we read how the people of God were called to remember all the good things the Lord had done for them. As you spend time in stillness of heart before the Lord, *first review your past.* Think back over your life and recall the times God has protected you, provided for you, blessed you, and cared for you.

*Second, reflect on the Lord Himself—on His greatness, on His grace, and on His goodness.* You may find it helpful as you do this to recall some of the names of God in the Bible—such as Jehovah, Yahweh, Elohim—that point to the nature of God as everlasting, infinite in power, absolutely faithful. *Finally, remember God's promises.* God's promises are for all of His children of every generation. He promises to provide for us and to work all things to our eternal good, protect us from evil, grant us His peace, forgive us of sin, give us His Spirit, and never to leave or forsake us.

The feelings associated with this step of meditation are usually joy, faith, an outpouring of love, thanksgiving, humility, praise, a positive feeling about the future, and an eagerness to see what God will do next.

**5.** How long did it take for you to get still before the Lord? What specific distractions did you encounter as you do this? (List those obstacles below so you can work on avoiding them in future times of meditation.)

...........................................................................

...........................................................................

...........................................................................

...........................................................................

...........................................................................

...........................................................................

**6.** What are some of the things the Lord brought to your mind during your time with Him? (Record them below and refer back to them in the coming days.)

...........................................................................

...........................................................................

...........................................................................

...........................................................................

...........................................................................

...........................................................................

# Making a Request
# and Submitting Your Will

So many of us rush to this phase of making a request of God. But it is more meaningful to make a petition to the Lord *after* you have entered into His presence with a committed heart and mind and removed the hindrances of sin or false understanding that might keep you from hearing Him clearly. Your requests are likely to be much different after you have spent time recalling God's work in your life. You will be far more likely to ask for the genuine desires of your heart, not mere superficial wishes.

As you take this step, state your request to God as simply as possible. Get to the very heart of what you want the Lord to do for you, in you, or through you. The feelings often associated with making a request are humility, release, and freedom. When you make an appropriate request before the Lord, you have a sense you are asking something the Lord desires for you. If you have to build a case for your request, you probably are asking in error.

Furthermore, as you make your request, be aware of any areas of pride in your heart. Ask God to remove that pride, and be aware of any lack of belief that God can and will answer your request. Be aware of any answers you are likely to reject out of hand even before God speaks. Ask Him to help you in your unbelief (see Mark 9:24).

Pray again the Lord will keep your mind open, unclouded, and uncluttered. Then sit before the Lord and wait for His response. The feeling one generally has at this point in meditation is a sense of giving up, surrendering, yielding, allowing, opening up, or receiving.

**7.** What genuine desires of your heart do you want to request from God? (Write these below, leaving room to write the Lord's answer and the date you receive the answer.)

**8.** In what ways do you sense you are making your request in accordance with God's will for your life? Were there any issues of pride you uncovered? Explain.

# GAINING A NEW PERSPECTIVE

When you meditate on the Lord, you will see things from a new perspective. The things that previously occupied your mind will lose their grip. New things will awaken in you. You will feel stronger and better able to face life. As we read in Psalm 36:9, "In Your light we see light." There is something about God shedding His light on a subject that causes you to see His truth.

The apostle Paul prayed that the Ephesians might be given a spirit of wisdom and revelation in the knowledge of God so they would know the hope of His calling, the riches of the glory of His inheritance, and the exceeding greatness of His power toward them (see Ephesians 1:17–18). What a wonderful thing to experience! Nothing will seem impossible to you if you come away with renewed hope, an awareness of all God has for you, and an assurance He can and will act in power to bring about all He has said.

Specifically, you can expect five feelings to pervade your entire being as the result of a time spent in meditation before the Lord. The first of these is *peace*. Jesus said, "My peace I give to you" (John 14:27). Christ's presence in you gives you a deep assurance and an abiding sense of rest. Your mind will no longer be tossed to and fro with wildly divergent opinions. Your heart will no longer feel troubled. Your spirit will no longer be agitated or feel pressed down under a heavy burden. You will know peace.

Second, you will experience a *positive attitude*. This is not simply positive thinking but an all-encompassing attitude that God is in charge and things are going to turn out according to His plan and purpose. A person with this attitude can't wait to get up the next day to see what God is going to do!

Third, you will experience *personal intimacy with God*. You will have a feeling after a time of deep meditation with the Lord that you have shared yourself fully with Him and that He has shared Himself fully with you. God is not detached, nor is He aloof or far away from you. In fact, He is nearer than near. He is within you . . . and you are within Him.

Fourth, you will experience *purification*. A time of sitting with the Lord will make you feel clean inside. The Lord's presence is purifying. The longer you are with Him, the more you will see yourself for who you are, the more willing you will be to face your sins and ask His forgiveness, and the greater the cleansing you will feel. With purification comes a feeling of release, freedom, and eagerness to move forward with strength.

Finally, you will experience a *passion to obey*. You can come before the Lord tired in body, weary in spirit, emotionally distraught, and fragmented in mind and find that after a time of meditation, you will feel energy, power, strength, and a renewed enthusiasm for life. God works from the inside out to refresh you. The result is that you have an eagerness to get up, get moving, and actually *do* what the Lord has revealed to you. You feel an eagerness to follow the Lord and receive all He has prepared for you. You want to do His will and walk in His ways because you know it will be for the glory of His name and for your eternal benefit.

God may not reveal His precise answer to you during your time of meditation, but you have the assurance He has heard your petition and His answer is on the way! You can feel confident that, as you continue to listen, you will hear all that He has to say to you. If you spend time with the Lord and don't experience these indicators, I encourage you to spend more time with Him. Go back and ask the Lord to reveal which step you may have missed or shortchanged in the process. Sit again in the Lord's presence—and do this as often as necessary until you feel peace, have a positive attitude, sense a deep personal intimacy with the Lord, are aware of inner purification, and have a passion to obey His word to you.

Now is the time to do this! If you are doing this study alone, identify a time and place you can shut yourself away with God to hear from Him. If you are doing this with a group, discuss with your fellow members how and when you will spend time with the Lord. Commit to making this a daily practice of sitting in God's presence and listening for His voice.

**9.** How did you experience a sense of *peace,* a *positive attitude, personal intimacy with God, purification,* and a *passion to obey* during your time with the Lord?

........................................................

........................................................

........................................................

........................................................

........................................................

........................................................

........................................................

........................................................

**10.** "Behold, I stand at the door and knock. If anyone hears My voice and opens the door, I will come in to him and dine with him, and he with Me" (Revelation 3:20). As you conclude this study, how do you sense God is knocking at the door of your heart? What is the promise in this verse if you choose to let Him in?

........................................................

........................................................

........................................................

........................................................

........................................................

........................................................

........................................................

........................................................

## TODAY AND TOMORROW

*Today:* Listening to God involves intimate times of conversation, as with a close friend.

*Tomorrow:* I will make it a priority to have daily appointments with God.

# CLOSING PRAYER

*Lord, You only speak to us with our best interests at heart. You only speak to us as a loving Father. We pray today, in Jesus' name, for anyone who is realizing for the first time that they are hearing Your voice and are under conviction that they need to surrender their lives to You. We also pray for those who have already made this decision that they would continue to seek You daily and meditate on Your Word. Thank You, Lord, that You allow us to come to You as we are—and that You are continually transforming us into the likeness of Your Son.*

# NOTES AND
# PRAYER REQUESTS

. . . . . . . . . . . . . . . . . . . . . . . . . . . . . . . . . . . . . . . . . . . .

Use this space to write any key points, questions, or prayer requests from this week's study.

# LEADER'S GUIDE

Thank you for choosing to lead your group through this Bible study from Dr. Charles F. Stanley on *Listening to God*. The rewards of being a leader are different from those of participating, and it is our prayer that your own walk with Jesus will be deepened by this experience. During the twelve lessons in this study, you will be helping your group members explore several key themes related to the topic of hearing God's voice through teachings by Dr. Charles Stanley and review questions that will encourage group discussion. There are multiple components in this section that can help you structure your lessons and discussion time, so please be sure to read and consider each one.

## BEFORE YOU BEGIN

Before your first meeting, make sure your group members each have a copy of *Listening to God* so they can follow along in the study guide and have their answers written out ahead of time. Alternately, you can hand out the study guides at your first meeting and give the group members some time to look over the material and ask any preliminary questions. During your first meeting, be sure to send a sheet around the room and have the members write down their name, phone number, and email address so you can keep in touch with them during the week.

To ensure everyone has a chance to participate in the discussion, the ideal size for a group is around eight to ten people. If there are more than ten people, break up the bigger group into smaller subgroups. Make sure the members are committed to participating each week, as this will help create stability and help you better prepare the structure of the meeting.

At the beginning of each meeting, you may wish to start the group time by asking the group members to provide their initial reactions to the material they have read during the week. The goal is to just get the group members' preliminary thoughts—so encourage them at this point to keep their answers brief. Ideally, you want everyone in the group to get a chance to share some of their thoughts, so try to keep the responses to a minute or less.

Give the group members a chance to answer, but tell them to feel free to pass if they wish. With the rest of the study, it's generally not a good idea to have everyone answer every question—a free-flowing discussion is more desirable. But with the opening icebreaker questions, you can go around the circle. Encourage shy people to share, but don't force them. Also, try to keep any one person from dominating the discussion so everyone will have the opportunity to participate.

## WEEKLY PREPARATION

As the group leader, there are a few things you can do to prepare for each meeting:

- *Be thoroughly familiar with the material in the lesson.* Make sure you understand the content of each lesson so you know how to structure the group time and are prepared to lead the group discussion.

- *Decide, ahead of time, which questions you want to discuss.* Depending on how much time you have each week, you may not be able to reflect on every question. Select specific questions you feel will evoke the best discussion.

- *Take prayer requests.* At the end of your discussion, be sure to take prayer requests from your group members and then pray for one another.

- *Pray for your group.* Pray for your group members through-out the week and ask that God would lead them as they study His Word.

- *Bring extra supplies to your meeting.* The members should bring their own pens for writing notes, but it's a good idea to have extras available for those who forget. You may also want to bring paper and additional Bibles.

# STRUCTURING THE GROUP DISCUSSION TIME

You will need to determine with your group how long you want to meet each week so you can plan your time accordingly. Generally, most groups like to meet for either sixty minutes or ninety minutes, so you could use one of the following schedules:

| SECTION | 60 Minutes | 90 Minutes |
|---|---|---|
| WELCOME (group members arrive and get settled) | 5 minutes | 10 minutes |
| ICEBREAKER (group members share their initial thoughts regarding the content in the lesson) | 10 minutes | 15 minutes |
| DISCUSSION (discuss the Bible study questions you selected ahead of time) | 35 minutes | 50 minutes |
| PRAYER/CLOSING (pray together as a group and dismiss) | 10 minutes | 15 minutes |

As the group leader, it is up to you to keep track of the time and keep things moving according to your schedule. If your group is having a good discussion, don't feel the need to stop and move on to the next question. Remember, the purpose is to pull together ideas and share unique insights on the lesson. Encourage everyone to participate, but don't be concerned if certain group members are more quiet. They may just be internally reflecting on the questions and need time to process their ideas before they can share them.

## GROUP DYNAMICS

Leading a group study can be a rewarding experience for you and your group members—but that doesn't mean there won't be challenges. Certain members may feel uncomfortable in discussing topics that they consider very personal and might be afraid of being called on. Some members might have disagreements on specific issues. To help prevent these scenarios, consider establishing the following ground rules:

- If someone has a question that may seem off topic, suggest that it is discussed at another time, or ask the group if they are okay with addressing that topic.

- If someone asks a question to which you do not know the answer, confess that you don't know and move on. If you feel comfortable, you can invite the other group members to give their opinions or share their comments based on personal experience.

- If you feel like a couple of people are talking much more than others, direct questions to people who may not have shared yet. You could even ask the more dominating members to help draw out the quiet ones.

- When there is a disagreement, encourage the members to process the matter in love. Invite members from opposing sides to evaluate their opinions and consider the ideas of the other members. Lead the group through Scripture that addresses the topic, and look for common ground.

When issues arise, encourage your group to follow these words from Scripture: "Love one another" (John 13:34), "If it is possible, as much as it depends on you, live peaceably with all men" (Romans 12:18), "Whatever things are true . . . noble . . . pure . . . lovely . . . if there is any virtue and if there is anything praiseworthy—meditate on these things" (Philippians 4:8), and "Be swift to hear, slow to speak, slow to wrath" (James 1:19). This will make your group time more rewarding and beneficial for everyone who attends.

Thank you again for your willingness to lead your group. May God reward your efforts and dedication, equip you to guide your group in the weeks ahead, and make your time together in *Listening to God* fruitful for His kingdom.

# Also Available in the
# Charles F. Stanley Bible Study Series

The Charles F. Stanley Bible Study Series is a unique approach to Bible study, incorporating biblical truth, personal insights, emotional responses, and a call to action. Each study draws on Dr. Stanley's many years of teaching the guiding principles found in God's Word, showing how we can apply them in practical ways to every situation we face. This edition of the series has been completely revised and updated, and includes two brand-new lessons from Dr. Stanley.

Advancing
Through Adversity
9780310106555

Experiencing
Forgiveness
9780310106579

Listening
to God
9780310106593

Relying on the
Holy Spirit
9780310106616

Available now at your favorite bookstore.
More volumes coming soon.

 THOMAS NELSON
Since 1798